Vicki Lansky's Divorce Book for Parents

Other titles by Vicki Lansky

Vicki Lansky's Divorce Book for Parents

Helping Your Children Cope with Divorce and Its Aftermath

NAL BOOKS

NEW AMERICAN LIBRARY

A DIVISION OF PENGUIN BOOKS USA INC., NEW YORK

PUBLISHED IN CANADA BY
PENGUIN BOOKS CANADA LIMITED, MARKHAM, ONTARIO

Published simultaneously in Canada by Penguin Books Canada Limited

Foreword by Hester Mundis reprinted with author's permission from "How to Survive a Divorce," *Working Mother*, May 1985

 NAL TRADEMARK REG. U.S. PAT. OFF. AND FOREIGN COUNTRIES
REGISTERED TRADEMARK—MARCA REGISTRADA
HECHO EN DRESDEN, TN, USA

SIGNET, SIGNET CLASSIC, MENTOR, ONYX, PLUME, MERIDIAN and NAL BOOKS are published in the United States by New American Library, a division of Penguin Books USA Inc., 1633 Broadway, New York, New York 10019 in Canada by Penguin Books Canada Limited, 2801 John Street, Markham, Ontario L3R 1B4

Library of Congress Cataloging-in-Publication Data

Lansky, Vicki.
 [Divorce book for parents]
 Vicki Lansky's divorce book for parents : helping your children cope with divorce and its aftermath / Vicki Lansky.
  p.   cm.
 Bibliography: p.
 Includes index.
 ISBN 0-453-00657-4
 1. Children of divorced parents. 2. Divorced parents.
I. Title. II. Title: Divorce book for parents.
HQ777.5.L36 1989
306.8'9—dc19   88-27227
                                                            CIP

Designed by Sherry Brown

First Printing, May, 1989

1 2 3 4 5 6 7 8 9

PRINTED IN THE UNITED STATES OF AMERICA

Contents

Acknowledgments

I only went through one divorce. To help with the wide range of variations experienced in divorce, I talked to many others and many read the manuscript in its various stages. Without all those other contributors, this book would not be what it is.

My thanks to all the divorced parents who took the time to read and comment on this manuscript: Susan Beatty, Carol Dickman, Gail Farber, MD., Nancy Frankenberry, Donna Gould, Karen Herrmann, Janie Jasin, Tamara Kaiser, Elliot Miller, Rod Martel, Heather Needleman, Andrea Posgay, Gabriel Poyton, Suzi Resnik, Toni Richards, Howard Rutman, Nancy Samalin, Susan Schulherr, Dorothy Skelly, Lisa Strom, Walter Tornow.

To the professionals in the area of helping families in transitions who went far beyond the traditional reading of a manuscript to make this book something special and something better:

Sally Brush, education and training coordinator of the Aring Institute, in Cincinnati

Dr. Gail Berkove, family therapist in Detroit

David Levy, Anna Keller, and John Bauserman of NCCR

Naomi Oxman, MSW, ACSW, psychotherapist with the University of Minnesota Department of Children and Adolescence and affiliated with Minneapolis Jewish Family Services

To those who assisted in special interest areas: Rabbi Norman Cohen, Ann Roberts and Bev Emshoff, June Tapp, Susan Shafer, Twila Ness, Henry Biller, Steve King, Lee Mauk.

To the lawyers who got me through my own divorce:

Les Novak and Tom Kaiser, who also read the legal section for me (and claim they have not billed me for).

To my agent and lawyer and friend, Neil Meyer, who edited the legal section of this book, as well as my publishing contract.

I couldn't have managed these many rewrites without the editorial help of Julie Surma and Sue Krajac, and special thanks for editorial work done by my editor and friend, Kathryn Ring, who also held my hand and listened to me *ad nauseum* during my own divorce. And to Alexia Dorszynski at New American Library, who not only saw to the book's publication, but improved the manuscript in the process.

To my children, Doug and Dana, for their insights, their presence, and for coming through our transition so wonderfully.

And to my ex, who never dreamed that he was giving me material for another book.

Foreword

THE VOICE OF EXPERIENCE

The best thing you can say about divorce is that it's a great Scrabble word. Other than that, divorce is the pits.

Untying the marital knots, like swimming down the Love Canal, ranks high among life's more unsavory passages. Though often referred to as a civil action, the process rarely is. Civilized divorce is a myth, and about as oxymoronic a term as any invented.

A first foray into divorce, especially when it's yours, is always the hardest. But a conjugal split, much like indigestion or a surprise visit from the in-laws, can happen to anyone—which is why if it happens to you, the most important thing to remember is to never take it personally.

—Hester Mundis, W. Shokan, NY

Preface

Getting divorced was not part of my long-term plan. My husband and I had participated in a business together, which he wished to run without me. I experienced the loss of my company, my spouse, and a traditional family life. I learned a lot about our legal system, too—more than I really wanted to know.

The divorce was not even my idea. I guess I never realized emotionally that it takes only one of the partners to start divorce proceedings. It took me a while to realize it was even happening to me. The experts call such an attitude "denial."

What's most amazing to me is the fact that my divorce was one of the best things that ever happened to me. It was also the worst thing that ever happened, and one of the most painful things. If anyone would have told me that it would be one of the best things for me—and come to think of it, I think they did—I would never have believed them. But it has been.

As a writer, I looked to the printed word, among other sources, to help me deal with what felt like the end of my life. I found helpful bits and pieces from many sources. But I'm a very nuts-and-bolts person, and it was hard to find the kind of information that I could use. My pattern has been to digest material that I've needed at different times in my life and put it together in a better format—one that would have been useful to me. That was how my first book, *Feed Me, I'm Yours*, a best-selling cookbook for babies and tots, and many of my subsequent books, came about. And that is also how this book evolved.

I knew early on that I wanted to put on paper ideas for coping with problems that I hadn't seen in other

books. I didn't do it right away. The first draft of this
manuscript started about two or three years after my
husband and I first separated, though I had been collecting everything written that I could find. The first
edition of this book was published on the sixth anni-
versary of my divorce.

No divorce is easy, and no two divorces are alike.
Many things in this book will not pertain to you because no two are alike. But I have tried to cover as
many of the combinations and permutations that I
know of by talking to other parents and having many
different people read the manuscript along the way.

I do not attempt to give legal advice. Instead, I hope
you will gain an insight into your situation, your options, a feeling of support, and at the same time, find
some useful ideas here.

You might think I'm painting a rather rosy picture
in this book and that the real world doesn't work like
this. But it *can*, and that's what you need to know.

—Vicki Lansky, April, 1989

Vicki Lansky's Divorce Book for Parents

1

The Decision to Separate

Once the decision to separate has been made, reality as well as numbness begins to wash over you. If you have found marriage painful, you're already becoming aware that separation and divorce will be even more so. Untangling the ties—and knots—of your marriage and your life as a couple is an experience unlike any you've ever had before. You're on uncharted waters and, whether you like it or not, you are the only true captain of your ship.

You may feel anger, sadness, anxiety, euphoria, depression, guilt, disorientation, fear, incompetence, shattered self-esteem, and rootlessness. The first weeks, months, or year are aptly named "crazy time" by one author. And it is.

Dr. E. Mavis Hetherington, Professor of Psychology at the University of Virginia, reports that most couples felt worse a year after the divorce than they had during the first few months. By then the novelty had worn off and the realities and loneliness had set in. I'm sharing the bad news first so that you will not be too hard on yourself during this difficult time—divorce is a stressful and painful transition. But, the good news is your life will improve—though probably not on a timetable of your choice. Be patient.

Where do you begin? Basically, with your children, because they *began* with you. Divorce may be hard on

1

a parent, but it's even tougher on kids. Because your children are part of your lives, you and your spouse will always be part of each other's lives, too. Divorce doesn't mean the disappearance of your former spouse, as it sometimes does for childless couples—and it shouldn't.

The other bit of good news is that evidence today dismisses the notion that the overall impact of divorce on children is inevitably negative and damaging. Yes, divorce has a major impact on children, but children are affected more by the *way* a family restructures itself and the *way* the feelings are handled afterward than by the divorce itself.

A study of eleven- to fifteen-year-olds by Dr. Nicolas Long of the University of Kansas Medical Center and research from the University of Georgia concluded that the amount parents argue after divorce strongly affects a child's adjustment. The suggested solution is to avoid arguing in front of your children about alimony, visitation, and parenting parameters. Research indicates that children most at risk are from families where conflict and anger continue, or where the absent parent is truly absent.

THE RESTRUCTURING OF YOUR FAMILY IS IN YOUR HANDS. DIVORCES DON'T WRECK CHILDREN'S LIVES. PEOPLE DO.

Although early studies focused on the inability of children and families to cope with divorce, we are now learning that most divorces do not routinely leave people angry and bitter. Before 1970 most research emphasized the deviant aspects of divorce. But researchers are discovering that reorganization has the potential for growth and happiness for all family members. We know that children can prosper in single-parent homes as well as in two-parent homes. Some children even become stronger by acquiring new coping skills. "Despite the emotional difficulties of living in a divorced family, many children of divorce grow up to be self-reliant and financially responsible young adults," says Judith Wallerstein, an authority on divorce at the University of California, Berkeley, and the executive director of the Center for the Family in Transition.

Dr. Constance Ahrons, from the University of Southern California's School of Social Work, questioned the traditional stereotypical view of divorce as dysfunctional in a 1985 study. Looking at parental patterns of cooperation, she found that of the divorced couples, 28 percent fell into her category of "Perfect Pals," 38 percent were "Cooperative Colleagues," 25 percent were "Angry Associates," and only 24 percent were "Fiery Foes." Only parents in this last group were totally uncooperative. She noted that the group with the least amount of stress and the overall most functional relationship was the "Cooperative Colleagues." This group was able to work out most of the tensions that arise in a productive manner. She sees an increasing trend for divorced couples to manage some kind of healthy relationship even if it takes five years.

THE DANGER OF CONTINUING CONFLICT

Studies completed by Dr. Joanne Rocklin, who works with divorcing couples, clearly show that whether the family is divorced or intact, continued parental conflict is the most harmful aspect to children of any age. Children whose parents frequently argue in front of them often are less socially competent than their peers and get lower grades in school.

Too often divorcing parents mistakenly expect conflict to disappear once they separate. In reality, fighting and anger often increase at this time, affecting children negatively and adding to the stress they feel. Keep in mind that the less conflict a child experiences, the better a child is able to adjust; the more conflict, the more difficult adjustment a child experiences. Children whose parents divorce and continue fighting, are, in effect, hit with a double whammy. Psychologist Rex Forehand at the University of Georgia feels that divorce is a plausible option if it leads to less parental fighting. One side-effect he has noted is that children unknowingly pick up their parents' patterns of conflict, often learning to handle problem situations through verbal or physical aggression.

Nurturing children well during a divorce is not easy. Your own loss and pain can overwhelm you at times. Yet, a positive restructuring of family life after divorce can result in satisfying new relationships, with all family members learning better emotional tools for coping with the future. And freed from the tensions of a difficult marriage, divorced parents often do a better job of parenting than they did while married.

Keep in mind the words of Mel Krantzler, leading divorce psychologist, in his best-selling book, *Creative Divorce* (see page 243).

Children are resilient. Short of actual neglect and physical abuse, children can survive any family crisis without permanent damage—and can grow as human beings in the process—if they can sense some continuity and loving involvement on the part of their parents.

Ending a marriage is not easy. Divorce may be commonplace today, but it is still difficult.

BREAKING THE NEWS

Once you and your spouse have discussed separation and know that it will happen, your most immediate concern should be about the what, where, when, and how of telling your children about your decision. Don't put it off.

Breaking the news to the kids could possibly be the toughest thing you've ever had to do. and it's an *absolute necessity* that they hear this from both of you—both their parents. Some parents renege on this painful responsibility, especially if their children are young. One parent may simply move out of the house, perhaps when the children are asleep. This will look and feel like desertion to a child. Researchers found in one study of preschool-age children of divorced parents that an almost unbelievable 80 percent had neither been forewarned about the departure nor told why it took place. Fear of total abandonment was extreme for these children; if one parent can leave home without explanation, might not the other parent, too?

Children deserve to hear the truth, no matter how painful it is. A child is never too young to understand. A child left in the dark can be devastated and will imagine things far worse than the truth. A child may become convinced the divorce is his or her fault. The message you send is that he or she is not important enough to be involved in serious family affairs. If a child hears about the divorce from the outside, he or she will most certainly feel betrayed.

Though I'm a therapist, I found talking to my three children around the time of my divorce absolutely terrifying. I had never felt so inadequate or alone. I had sense enough to follow the old adage, "When in doubt, tell the truth." To that I added my variation, "Never lie, but the whole truth isn't always helpful." I answered every question asked by my children to the best of my ability but discovered most questions asked by them were easily answered. 'Where will I live? When will we see you? Will I still get my allowance?'

—Larry Meyers, Santa Ana, CA

For the Kids' Sake

Whatever your differences may be, can you and your spouse agree that you don't want to hurt your children? Will you and your spouse work together to make the process as easy as possible for them?

When the decision has been made to separate, even the most caring parents are not totally rational. It's hard to be fully supportive and available to your children's emotional needs at this time. Don't be too hard on yourself if you make some mistakes along the way. Genuine consideration and concern will make up for the rough spots.

It's important that you and your spouse thoroughly review what will be said to the children beforehand, if at all possible. Prepare for this meeting very carefully. To reduce the children's anxiety, give them only enough information to explain the situation; try not to overburden them with details. Consider your children's ages and developmental stages. Discuss with each other the importance of keeping the children out of your legal and financial differences. Try to reach agreement with each other on as many things as possible before approaching the kids.

Even though one parent has rejected a life together with the other parent, this doesn't mean that either he or she is not a good or capable parent. In other words, if your spouse has ended your marriage, that is not a reason for you to end his or her parenting.

Of the following list of considerations, a discussion

of custodial arrangements is the most important. It is vital to come to a general understanding about how you wish to handle your children's living arrangements and your parenting time. Your unofficial temporary custody schedule will also lay the ground rules for your future arrangements. Separation is a temporary but significant period that is a legal no-man's-land—a time of informal arrangements. Think through your plans as clearly as is possible. From the beginning of your separation period, before the divorce is final, you and your spouse can experiment with different custodial configurations, testing, so to speak, the *custodial waters*. Discuss the fact that you will both remain open to changes to any initial arrangement but not to such a degree that it may confuse the children.

Child-related Considerations to Discuss Beforehand

- When will we tell the children?
- Will we tell them together?
- What will we tell them?
- Who will tell them what?
- How should time with the children be shared?
- How should the holidays be handled?
- How should religious education be dealt with?
- Who will be a primary custodial parent?
- Where will the children live?
- Where will the other parent live?
- When will the departing parent move out?
- How will continuing contact with the children be handled?

Trial Separations

If this is to be a trial separation, your children have a right to know this. You and your spouse owe it to each other to discuss the separation and what it means

before announcing it to your children. You'll need to
discuss your own "rules of the road."

In addition to the considerations just listed, think
about:

- Are there any clear preconditions for a reunion?
  Children should be told that it is not *their* behavior
  that will determine a reunion.
- If either of you date or have other relationships,
  will this stand in the way of a reconciliation?
- Are you willing to "date" each other, now or later?

Planning Your Words

Be aware that the unknown frightens children more
than the known, however unpleasant it may be. Kids'
thoughts naturally center around themselves. Thus,
they worry first about what will happen to *them*. The
greatest fear that most children have is that when
some things change, *all* things will change. Be prepared to tell them as clearly as you can about how
things will be after the separation and to assure them
that they will be cared for, protected, and loved by
both parents, if it is true.

- Make a checklist of the questions and issues you
  want to discuss with your spouse; try to think of
  everything the children could possibly ask—or won't
  ask—but should know.
- Agree that you will not use this explanation of your
  divorce as an excuse for an argument between you
  and your spouse.
- If there is a personal or intimate problem that is
  inappropriate for discussion, you might both agree to
  a response that there are some private reasons that
  Mommy and Daddy can't discuss but have nothing
  to do with children and are "adults only" problems.

• If substance abuse is part of the problem, avoid describing the other parent as "bad." Instead, discuss what you do not like about your spouse's behavior and its effect on you.

Picking a Time and Place

Ideally, you and your spouse will arrange when and where you will tell the children. This is not always a rational process or a planned event, but if you can make it one, if you have time to prepare, keep these thoughts in mind:

• Choose a time convenient for both of you to talk with the children. Make this time long enough before one parent moves out to give adequate notice, but not so far ahead that the children will think the separation will not take place. Do not have a discussion of divorce and separation unless the decision is final; living in uncertainty and worry is as hard on children as it is adults.
• Make a firm commitment not to argue before or during the talk so that you can approach this important time calmly and reasonably. Be honest, but try to control your emotions.
• Plan to be together to tell the children if at all possible, even if one of you will do most of the talking. Children will probably have questions to ask both of you, and you owe it to them to be there to answer them. If you absolutely cannot tell them as a team, discuss together what each parent will say, so that the children will not be further confused with different stories. Have your first talk with all your children as a group, even if they are widely separated in age. Being together will help them all. There will be time later to explain more fully to those who are old enough to know more and to comfort each individually.

• Write down your words afterward (or even before, if you wish) and give your children a backup, written explanation for them to refer to as it fits their needs.

If you know that telling the children separately is really the best way for your family or it has just happened that way, then that is how it will be. There is no perfect way to do this difficult task.

Break the news at home, not as part of an outing. Be sure the TV is off. Allow enough time to explain what you have to say and to answer any questions your children have. Don't rush through the talk; give children time to air feelings and mull over the implications. Be sure to convey hope rather than despair. Earlier in the day is probably better than later in the day, but the chances are no one will sleep very well that night, anyway.

Over the next few days you might find that you will have additional sessions as questions arise.

> FIRST, LAST, AND ALWAYS,
> CHILDREN HAVE A RIGHT TO
> HAVE, TO BE WITH, AND
> TO LOVE . . . BOTH PARENTS.

If the Departure Isn't Planned

Be honest with your children. If the move took place when they weren't there, or if your spouse left in the middle of the night, tell them it was a *real* move, not that "Daddy's going to be on a business trip for a few days" or "Mommy's gone to visit Grandma." A lie will only require further explanations later and cause the children more confusion and anxiety.

If one parent has asked the other to leave or had him (her) removed because of fear of physical harm, it is important to explain this to children. If the leave-taking involves an angry scene or a display of other strong emotions that the children witness, try to explain it as rationally and as calmly as you can later, however upset you may be. The departed parent should be urged to write or call the children immediately to help them understand this sudden change and to establish contact.

Children can also be encouraged to write down their feelings or write a letter to the other parent to set up an "in contact" situation. Even very young children can "dictate" such a letter. It is an opportunity for your child to vent feelings; and you can help it to not be a guilt trip on the other parent, but rather a bridge to future contact.

Telling the Kids

Saying the words, "We're getting a divorce" to your children has been compared to shouting, "Fire!" in a crowded theater. It will be your job to reassure your children and convince them that their best interests will always be uppermost in both of your minds.

To children, parents are a package deal, not two adults with different views and values. Your children never knew you when you had prior lives apart. Parents represent a whole and a complete universe. Now you are telling them that you will be splitting something that they feel is indivisible.

FOR YOU, AS WELL AS FOR
YOUR CHILDREN, THERE IS NO
PAIN MORE AWFUL THAN
BEING LEFT OR FORCED TO
LEAVE SOMEONE YOU LOVE.

Select your words carefully. Speak in language appropriate to your children's level of understanding. But, just as a doctor warns that a shot will hurt, be honest about the pain that's involved, for your children and for you and your spouse as well.

- Don't pretend it's unimportant or make light of it. It might ease your guilt to think you won't upset your kids, but news of their parents' divorce is serious information to them, and you will confuse them by not treating it seriously.
- For children who are not familiar with the word, explain that divorce means that one parent will be moving out of their home and each parent will live in a separate home. They may also need explanations of the words *lawyer, custody, divorce stipulation,* and *going to court.*
- Explain what will concern the children most—their future living arrangements. Tell them as much as you can about where they will live, where the departing parent will live, and when they will spend time with each parent.
- If you know you will be offering your children two homes in a shared parenting arrangement, let them know these plans. But don't imagine for a minute that this is a positive selling point ("Lucky you, now you'll have two homes instead of just one") when you present the idea.
- Explain the details you know about expected changes. Be honest about conflicts, but don't elaborate on those that may cause anxiety, such as money. One piece of devastating news at a time is enough. (The threat of money problems may make kids feel guilty and think that if it weren't for them, your married life would continue without problems.)
- Let your children know that there are many different kinds of loving. The feelings between a man and woman are not the same as the feelings a parent has for a child, even though we use the word *love* to describe both.

- Be honest, but don't make excuses for the other parent in order to minimize a child's pain. Just as it is important not to attack the other parent, don't err in the other direction by covering for that parent, either.
- Explain that you and your spouse cannot live together any longer, but that your separating is in no way the fault of any child.
- If you've had marital therapy, let the children know that you tried but still couldn't improve your relationship.
- Don't lie to your children. The truth often comes out eventually and they will resent you for hiding it. You risk losing their trust and could damage their trust for adults in general.
- Let the children know they will be kept informed about changes that concern them. If there is the possibility of a major change, such as a move or change of school, they'll need to know. No one likes changes, especially ones that they have no control over, but adjustment and acceptance are more positive when there has been advance warning.
- Avoid blaming your spouse for the dissolution of your marriage and home life in front of the children. Every divorce is subject to this attack. It's tempting—in every divorce there is usually one who "wants" the divorce initially—but avoid it.
- Let your children hear of your love for them. And, most important, let them know you wish that their love for the other parent will continue and can grow.
- Don't make promises you can't keep.
- If one parent has concrete plans to move in with a lover, the children's living options will obviously be affected. It's best to answer truthfully rather than risk loss of trust by avoiding the subject. Hopefully,

the exiting parent will not make this type of move initially; this can be particularly confusing and difficult for children.)

In some families, one parent may be immobilized and all this responsibility may fall to the other parent. Despite feelings of numbness and confusion on the part of that parent, the children are entitled to share in and know about the changes in their family. And remember it's important that children be told firmly that you *will* separate and that your plans to do so are *final*.

Give a Reason for Your Divorce

Children need to know why the divorce is occurring so they don't blame themselves. Finding the right words is not always easy.

Be sure your children are told:

> THEY DID NOT CAUSE THE
> DIVORCE . . . NOR COULD THEY
> HAVE PREVENTED IT!

Your tone and your words make a difference. Try to explain the reasons without anger and harshness in your voice. If a parent is ill (because of alcoholism, drug addiction, or mental illness), a child needs to be told. Sometimes the ill parent is not yet receiving treatment (or even seeking it), but that parent's "illness" can still be discussed in age-appropriate words. ("Daddy/Mommy is in the hospital because he/she's not feeling well and needs special help to talk about what is bothering him/her.") Such illnesses may prevent that parent from showing love and concern for a child, and this knowledge will help any children.

If your household has been noisy and combative,

these outward signs make it easier for children to understand that reasons may exist. On the other hand, if you don't fight and seem to have a calm and cooperative relationship with the other parent, then children may be at a loss to understand why you must divorce. They will need help understanding that:

- Not all anger is noisy anger.
- Adult sexual preferences and outside opposite sex relationships change the nature of a marriage for adults.
- Not all adults share the same values in families, and such differences sometimes cause families to restructure.
- The purpose of the divorce is to try to make things better for one or both adults.

You might not yet truly understand the real reasons for your own divorce. Often these only reveal themselves with time. The apparent reasons or the symptomatic reasons will do as an explanation for now.

While putting Christopher to bed one night, we were talking about our separation and ultimate divorce. Rich and I had agreed to use the "Mom and Dad don't love each other anymore" approach and say that our arguments were part of the reason. Out of the blue he asked,"Is it my fault?" I had to quickly gather my composure and tell him it was not his fault and had nothing to do with him. I was astounded that even a twenty-seven month-old child could assume so much responsibility.
— *Karyn Herrmann, Minneapolis, MN*

Even if you think the reason you're divorcing is because you and your spouse have "fallen out of love" with each other, don't tell this to your children. Aside from the fact

that it will cause children to fear that you'll fall out of love with them, it's not the whole truth—and if you don't know that, you're the one who needs talking to.
                                        —Hester Mundis, W. Shokan, NY

AFTER YOU'VE BROKEN THE NEWS

Don't be surprised if a child appears to take your news lightly and perhaps even shows signs of impatience to get away. Denial and disbelief are common responses. Some children operate on the "If you don't look at it, it will go away" premise. Your child may even express relief at first, feeling grateful there will be no more fighting in the house, but not fully realizing both parents will no longer be available simultaneously. Most, however, will be opposed to a divorce and will be angry and feel scared or anxious. Once over the shock, they may cry, though it may be hours or days later.

You would never consider performing an appendectomy on a child without anesthetic, but we do 'Parent-ectomies' on kids every day.
                              —Dr. Frank Williams, psychiatrist and director of
                                  Thalians Community Mental Health Center, CA

Listen!

Listen carefully to the kids' responses, to be sure they are not misinterpreting your meanings, especially about the possibility of your reuniting. Respond to their feelings, not just to their words.

- Allow the children to show their grief after you've broken the news. There may be tears, denial, pleas for reconsideration, curses, threats, false bravado, or silence. Be sure both you and your spouse show your love by holding or hugging them, if they let you. Being upset is part of what children must go through. Let them know that all these feelings are okay.
- If the child expresses strong feelings of anger toward you, avoid expressing anger in return. It's important to let your child express these strong feelings without fear of losing your love.
- If your children don't want to talk about the divorce or share their emotions with you initially, let it go for a little while. You're more likely to hurt than help if you force thoughts and feelings a child is not ready to confront. The truth is, the child might not yet know how he or she actually does feel. A period of denial can be a helpful coping mechanism as a short-term response in stressful situations.
- Let children know you're available to listen or to clarify any of their questions whenever they are interested in talking.
- After a few weeks, try asking a preschooler who's reluctant to talk to draw a picture about how your family looks now that a separation will (or has) occurred. Ask for explanations of what you see in the picture, and use it as a point of discussion as to why he or she thinks the divorce happened. This may help uncover any false impressions.
- Ask an older child to write a story about his or her feelings if you think they're being held in.
- Encourage a child to talk to an appropriate third party who may be less involved, such as a teacher, baby-sitter, or relative.

Sometimes children say nothing because they don't want to hurt you. Children often want to protect their parents and will keep their feelings inside as one way to avoid making things worse for their parents. If, after a time, you find you have gotten little feedback on their feelings, perhaps it will help if you share some of your feelings first. It's possible to share some of your pain and concern without it being a burden to your children, and it often gives them permission to open up. They will be confused if you show no emotion and they may feel as if they must be stoic, too.

Kids don't always have the vocabulary they need to talk about their feelings. Words you suggest might fill in their blanks. "Feeling empty" will put more common words to the feeling we know as depression; "hurting" is a grieving expression.

Allow your children time to adjust—a lot of time. Understand that there is a real difference between parents and kids making adjustments. After all, one parent, if not both, have been thinking about this change for quite awhile. For most kids, it's all brand new. Be patient with an unhappy child.

It's hard to accept a child's anger and hurt while you are feeling your own sense of loss and/or guilt over the divorce. Divorce tends to invalidate your own feelings of worth. It's so tempting to try to get your sense of self-worth or validation for your righteous indignation from your children. Kids often sense this and come to the rescue . . . but usually at a cost to themselves.

REMEMBER: CHILDREN DO NOT BELIEVE IN NO-FAULT DIVORCE. THEY BLAME ONE OR BOTH PARENTS, OR THEY BLAME THEMSELVES.

All parents feel that to some degree they have failed their kids with the breakup of a marriage. Realize that these feelings are perfectly normal for you, too.

My parents separated when I was twelve. It damaged my self-image. Nobody ever explained why the divorce was taking place, and I always felt I was to blame.
   —Adrienne Barbeau, actress, Reseda, CA

The Value of Crying

Tears are part of the human condition. All people should be permitted to cry when sad. Crying relieves tension and helps us cope with emotional loss. We now know that not allowing oneself to cry can relate to future health problems and contribute to stress-related problems.

Crying is never a sign of weakness for either a child or an adult. It hurts to be rejected or left by someone you love, and crying is an honest and natural reaction to this kind of pain. Tears are a necessary part of "letting go."

- Restrain yourself from saying things like, "Don't cry. Everything will be all right."
- Don't deny a youngster the opportunity to cry. Don't worry if you don't know what to say. A hug or silent companionship is often all that's needed as your response.

- Crying together as a family can be a form of support and confirmation of everyone's sadness and loss.
- Each parent and child's need to cry publicly or privately is different.

On moving-out day, my daughter saw her father break down and cry several times. I hadn't realized she had never seen him cry before, and it was very hard on her. I tried to help her see that when something is hard on you, you do cry. I told her that I had seen her father cry before and I was glad he was the kind of honest man who could show his feelings.

—Unsigned

Children often feel that they can't tell parents they've been crying. Many just don't know how to approach parents who now may appear wrapped up in their own problems. Letting children know that you cry privately may give a child "permission" to share the same information with you.

"Parents who cover up their feelings actually make their children's adjustment more difficult," says Sally Brush of the Aring Institute in Cincinnati, Ohio, which offers support services to divorcing families. Kids get permission to grieve partly by seeing their parents grieve. If parents are expressing their own feelings adequately, children don't have to grieve for their parents but can concentrate on their own grief.

Because we find it difficult to see our children in pain, we are tempted to give superficial reassurances: "Oh, honey, it's all right. You'll be fine. Things will be better soon." Because it takes a long time for "things to be better," by saying this you will lose credibility; kids aren't sure you understand the depth of their pain.

Important Daily Reassurances, Repetitions, and Affirmations

Children of all ages need constant reassurance that their lives will not be ruined and that certain facts and feelings will not change. They need to know they can count on you. Tell them seriously and often, because it takes time for this to sink in.

"You are not responsible *in any way* for the divorce."

"We are divorcing each other; we are not divorcing you."

"We are sad that this is happening, and we are sorry about it for your sake and for ours."

"You will always be cared for and protected."

"You are not going to be asked to take sides with either parent."

"Our decision to separate has been made; you cannot change that."

"The fact that Mom and Dad aren't suited for each other any longer doesn't mean that we aren't suited to be your parents. We can be a mother and father to you without being husband and wife to each other."

"Even good parents get divorced, and we can continue being good parents to you."

"We seem to have problems we just can't work out. We both feel badly about it."

"We loved each other when you were born. We loved you when you were born and we love you now. That will never change."

"Feelings of love between adults can change, but the lasting bond between a parent and child is a different and special kind of love."

"Neither Mom nor Dad will ever stop loving you, however faraway either of us may live."

"You may find this painful and difficult now, but you will feel better again. Happiness is down the road. Trust me."

TELLING THE OTHERS

Informing friends and family of your decision will
seem much easier than telling your children, because
their lives will not be affected as strongly as your
kids'. The news may not be totally unexpected by
adults you have confided in or who were aware of
your stressful marriage. When possible:

- Inform everyone who should know about your separation in person, by phone, or by letter. However
  reluctant you feel about it, explanations will not be
  easier later. Avoid the embarrassment and confusion (for yourself and others) that are sure to result
  if they hear the news from someone else.
- If a reconciliation is a possibility, you may want to
  share that. If divorce is inevitable, say so. Verbalizing what is happening helps you become more accustomed to it, too.
- Consider using your annual holiday letter to spread
  the news to those who live faraway and whom you
  don't see often.
- Avoid discussing all the unpleasant details of your
  divorce with friends and family members who wish
  to remain neutral; that way they don't feel so com-
  pelled to take sides. You need to talk about your
  anger and frustration, but some of those who are
  close to you may not be the appropriate outlets.
- Be aware that you will have friends who will choose
  to be friends with both of you. You may find yourself angry or hurt with some for not "siding" with
  you—despite the fact that you may have said, "I
  understand you'd like to be friends with both of
  us."
- Be prepared for the extra sadness of losing some
  friends. Some married friends have trouble befriend-

ing a single person. You can threaten their own marriage. Others will gravitate toward your spouse. Some slip away as your life-style changes. You may never know why some of your friends just pull away.

- Don't forget to inform other significant adults in a child's life, such as baby-sitters and neighbors, who will be supportive of the children and better able to deal with any behavioral changes that might occur.

The only thing harder than telling your kids is telling your parents. The news can be a shock and a tremendous disappointment to them. Parents and in-laws may feel deceived or embarrassed. You can tell them as a couple, or individually. It is natural to look to your own family to "side" with you, but give your parents permission to continue their relationship with your exiting spouse and family.

I felt like a failure telling my parents. I was the first in a family of six children to get a divorce.
                                    —Margaret Leduc, Romulus, MI

The breakup of a marriage does not mean that all family relationships must simultaneously and auto-matically dissolve. If you have been on friendly terms with your in-laws, get in touch with them as soon as your decision to separate is final, even if your spouse has already done so, to lay the groundwork for "keep-ing the doors open."

Remember that your spouse's parents will always be your children's grandparents and that their continued relationship with the kids may offer stability in a time of uncertainty. Unless they are alcoholic or abusive, it's important to work at letting the grandparent/

grandchild relationship grow. Reassure grandparents they will not lose contact with their grandchildren—then see that they don't. A divorce is a loss for them, and grandparents need to maintain close relationships with their grandchildren (see page 208).

Let your own parents know what kind of help you want from them—emotional, practical (like baby-sitting), financial, or whatever. Many adult children have to move home for a time. Be specific in your requests for help. Not all will be accommodated, but it's worth the risk of asking.

"Do I Offer Congratulations or Condolences?"

Telling others about your divorce is uncomfortable for them. People don't know what to say. A quick follow-up comment on your part can help put the other person in a better position as to how they can respond. You can say, "We're separating and (a) I had to ask him/her to leave; (b) I was as surprised as you are; (c) it was a hard decision but a mutual one; or (d) !*&#)!!**@!$!"

A LOOK AT THE BRIGHTER SIDE

As difficult as this transition will be there are certain advantages that you will experience along the way. On your darkest days keep these in mind:

• You have crossed the biggest bridge—that of change. The fear of impending change is often worse than the change itself.

• Your house will be quieter. If there was constant fighting and exposure of raw emotions, this will end.

- You will no longer be walking on eggshells. Your home can become a haven and a refuge rather than a place you'd rather not be. You won't be criticized or traumatized.
- Family relationships will be simplified. You'll have less "covering," less coping to do.
- If you've lived with the unpredictable behavior of a spouse who's chemically dependent, your life will become more stable.
- You'll discover you are really not so worthless after all!
- Single parenting means doing what you want to do, rather than what you thought you "should" do in conjunction with your spouse. If you don't care if the toys get picked up or not, now it doesn't matter. You can also get that pet your spouse was allergic to.
- Circumstances may push your kids into becoming more self-sufficient and responsible. The result might well be increased self-esteem.
- You'll have time now to develop and rekindle same-sex friendships, especially those your spouse never cared for.
- Decision making and creating your own style become habit forming and even rather pleasant. You can eat what you like, travel when and where you wish, and budget according to your priorities.
- Your closet space will increase.
- You will discover a whole new world of things you are quite capable of doing for yourself and by yourself.
- You can sleep in the middle of the bed, watch TV as late as you like, get crumbs on the bedsheets, and use the bathroom in privacy anytime you want— unless you have teenagers, that is.

Laugh Through Your Tears

Breaking Up: From Heartache to Happiness, by
Yolanda Nave, 48 pages, Workman $3.50.

This delightful cartoon book begins with THE END
and ends with THE BEGINNING. If it doesn't seem
funny now, it will twelve months from today.

*See page 244.

And the Not-So-Bright Side

Before your family reorganizes, it will disorganize.
Adults usually underestimate the difficulty of this transition and the length of time—often several years—
before there is enough new stability to provide comfort
and a renewed sense of future.

Divorces aren't always entered into by two cooperat-
ing people, so all divorces aren't always smooth for
parents or children. One parent can't "do" a divorce
alone. This translates to: You won't always be able to
make it best for your kids, despite how much understanding and how many terrific communication skills
you possess. All you can do is your half and keep
reciting the Serenity Prayer.

Serenity Prayer

*God Grant Me the Serenity to Accept the Things I
Cannot Change,
The Courage to Change the Things I Can,
and
The Wisdom to Know the Difference.*

Lots of little things will fall to you alone, now. You'll be the last one turning off the lights at night. You'll be taking out the garbage yourself, for example, rather than sharing duties with a spouse. There are many harder things you will encounter:

- Facing your financial future alone will be scary in the beginning.
- Your life-style will probably change. Single-parent families or the divided resources of a family with joint custody often cause a drop in income, which can and usually does place an added stress on children.
- Your spouse may not be comfortable sharing parenthood because of feelings of loss of control—real or imagined. Unfortunately, there are also parents who do not care about cooperation, sharing, or being supportive.
- A competitive parent may carry this trait over into a divorce so that power and winning on one or more fronts may become a major part of your divorce.
- There's no one to share good news with.
- The new aloneness can be painful for a long time. (Times does temper this, however.)

Litigation, fair representation, and fair play are not always possible when money is limited. And not always then, either.

For adults, divorce can exhaust, demoralize, bankrupt, and alienate.

FOR CHILDREN, THERE IS SELDOM A BRIGHTER SIDE TO A DIVORCE.

When We Are Flat on Our Backs, There Is No Where to Look But Up.

—R. W. Babson

2

How Will the Children Take It?

Psychologists say divorce is only slightly less traumatic for children than the death of a parent. In many cases, both come as a total shock, but in death, mourning is accepted and encouraged, and friends and relatives are usually available to help and console both adults and children. But in the crisis of divorce, the support of family and parents is usually not available to children. Often parents themselves are unable to cope and are unavailable to parent their children adequately. In addition, parents may keep their sadness to themselves, thinking they are sparing their children; in reality this can prevent children from going through the normal grieving period that helps relieve sorrow. According to a report in *Pediatric News* (June 1985) the "normal" mourning process for children ranges from four to twelve weeks. This time frame refers to the initial grief. Mourning symptoms include angry outbursts, low energy, crying, and constant questioning. Other research suggests that the total mourning process is best measured in terms of months and sometimes years—not weeks.

You may wonder why children grieve—shouldn't they be relieved, especially if they have witnessed fighting between parents? Remember, many children are happy in their intact family life even when the parents are unhappy. The grief children can feel does not necessarily correspond with how close the parent and child were, so expect mourning even if you saw your child's relationship with the other parent as minimal. Yet the closer attachment a child has to a now-distanced parent, the harder it will be for that child.

WHAT YOU CAN EXPECT

According to researchers Wallerstein and Kelly in the California Children of Divorce Project, children's reactions to learning about separation and divorce are:

- Shock, surprise, and disbelief
- Worry about how their world will change
- Sadness and loneliness
- Shame and feeling different
- Anger at both parents
- Confusion over loyalty

These feelings follow the general stages of grief in the death and dying process as outlined by Elizabeth Kubler-Ross in her watershed work, *On Death and Dying*. The last steps in this process are mourning the loss and, finally, acceptance. But divorce, unlike death, makes the departed parent simultaneously both unavailable and available.

Being reasonably candid about problems with children old enough to understand and admitting your sorrow that the marriage is over will help them through the grieving stage. Resolving old grievances between you and your spouse and settling money and custody issues as smoothly and as quickly as possible will help everyone get on with their new lives.

Some children protect their emotional side by turning off their feelings. The apprehension most children experience regarding the uncertainty that lies ahead greatly outweighs any relief they may feel at the ending of an angry marriage. Recognize these feelings of ambivalence in your children, realize they will feel both angry and relieved, and let them know that their reactions are okay.

Children who show few feelings are not necessarily more or less troubled than children who appear more openly distressed. Remember, the way grief is expressed does not necessarily correspond to the way it's felt. Most children will see their parents' divorce as the single major trauma of their childhood.

Although research does suggest that divorce hurts many children at least for a time, it is wrong to conclude that all children have significant problems or that all children experience difficulty equally. The extent to which children are affected varies and effects will be determined by not one, but several factors. Your child's reactions will depend on economic circumstances, ages, gender, personalities, repertoire of coping skills, the nature of your family, degree of continued access to both parents, the presence of a third party, and the degree of hostility expressed. Your children's reactions will be determined to a large degree by your reaction. Children will model their behavior on how you are coping.

HOW WELL YOU HANDLE THE
DIVORCE TRANSITION AND
YOUR OWN ANGER WILL AFFECT
YOUR CHILDREN FAR MORE THAN
THE DIVORCE ITSELF.

Children's behavioral problems can be altered or reduced when parents respond to children with age-appropriate actions and words.

The best way you can help your children is to take care of yourself, and to avoid showing open hostility to the other parent. No matter how difficult your spouse may be, remember: A fight requires at least two people!

Children thrive on stability and routine. By contrast, insecurity and anxiety are the normal reactions during the flurry of changes during separation and divorce. The more you can do to keep a stable base for your children, the better they will do. Maintaining a routine is one way to reduce uncertainty and reassure kids that their world isn't falling apart. Each family's routines are unique; whatever yours have been, do your best to continue them.

I maintained a structured daily schedule for my three-and-a-half-year-old daughter. We kept up connections with former friends, ate familiar foods, and I spent a lot of quality time with her that first year. We did have to change residences. Years later she shared her anger about our moving from a house to an apartment.

—Susan Resnik, New York City

Interestingly, it appears that it is fairly common for the parent initiating the divorce to perceive the children as doing just fine, whereas the abandoned parent perceives the children as troubled or damaged.

What to Do About "WHYS?"

You will probably be faced many times with the question, "Why?" from your child(ren). Why? covers a lot of whys. *Why me? Why us? Why don't you love me enough to make this marriage work? Why is this really happening? Why can't we all live together again?* If you have been truthful with your children and yet they keep asking for the *real* story behind your divorce, they may actually be asking these hidden questions:

Was I responsible?
Will you leave me next?
Will you always love me?

One round of reassurance on your part is not enough. Your children will need many more rounds.

Listening to "Why did you make Daddy/Mommy leave?" is very painful. You must remind yourself that you are the adult. Your child cannot possibly share your perspective. Your child's reactions are just those—a child's reactions. Part of your job as an adult will be to handle your feelings in an adult, mature fashion. No small job, I know. But acknowledging your child's feeling of sadness, anger, or frustration is your best response when your rational ones are not accepted.

AGE MAKES A DIFFERENCE

Your children's ages will be the major factor determining what reactions you can expect, what behavioral changes may occur, and how you can help each of your children. Your explanation and choice of words when explaining your divorce will differ, too, for a 2-year-old and a 12-year-old. You should consider each child's level of understanding, any prior knowledge of divorce that he or she has, and his or her gender.

However, some problems seem to be almost universal among children of all ages. Guilt is one, but although an adolescent may wonder and ask if he or she has caused your separation, a younger child will often simply assume responsibility for it and require repeated reassurance.

Having fewer past memories, very young children

Best Help for Children of Any Age

- Reassure your child that this separation is not his or her fault.
- Don't talk negatively or with anger about your spouse to your children on a regular basis. If you can't talk positively, limit what you say. It's okay to acknowledge your anger as long as your children understand they can and do have feelings that are different than yours.
- Try to avoid arguing bitterly in front of the kids so they won't feel that differences are resolved by yelling and fighting. Remember, too, that retreat and silence are just quieter forms of anger and are just as destructive.
- See if you can agree with your spouse about disciplinary matters, at least in the presence of your children.
- Make special efforts to maintain individual relationships with each child.
- Assure your child that it's okay to love the absent parent. A child who wants to be like Mom or Dad isn't being disloyal to you.
- Don't compare your child to your ex-spouse, even when similarities are poignantly striking and painful to observe.
- Don't blame your child's anxieties, fears, or problems at this difficult time on the absent parent—either to the child or the absent parent.
- Help your children not to feel shame about your divorce. If you feel shame and shut your children out, they too will be ashamed and worry about facing their friends and schoolmates. A divorce doesn't make you a failure.

- Don't make your child a messenger between you and your ex. Children will not enjoy being in the middle but they will probably not tell you that.
- Do let your children's teachers know about the change in your family's structure so they can help your child.
- Don't make too many changes in your child's life at once.
- Allocate family chores in such a way as to not overburden each child. Find ways to get house chores completed despite the absence of the one who *always* mowed the lawn, washed the car, and so on. Kids should not have to do all of Daddy's or Mommy's jobs around the house.
- Don't ask a child who she or he wants to live with or loves more . . . directly or indirectly!
- Encourage your child to resume normal activities.
- Acknowledge children's deep-seated wish for a reunited family without offering false hope or angry denials.
- Include a child in any appropriate discussions with a parent who will be making a long-distance move.
- Try to maintain as much emotional control as you can. If you repeatedly fall apart, your children may, too, or they may feel obligated to take over adult roles that are beyond them.
- Don't turn your child into your *adult* confidante.

And for yourself, forgive yourself if you haven't scored 100 percent on this list. No one does.

adapt faster to the new realities and tend to be less upset than preschoolers. A preschooler doesn't fully understand the implications of a separation and divorce but will still understand the absence of a parent and usually has a fear of abandonment. Children ages seven to eight will be sad and, in the event of a new significant other entering the picture or remarriage, will be fearful of being displaced in the family. A nine- or ten-year-old will be angry and feel victimized by an event over which he or she has no control, whereas an adolescent may be angry at the parent who he sees as the culprit and embarrassed by the whole situation. In their natural egocentricity, most children will worry about how their lives will be changed. Where will they live? Will they have to change schools? Will they still go on vacations or away to camp? What will happen if one parent moves far away or remarries?

It's common at any age for children to take sides, based on often incorrect observations or biased words of one or the other parent.

One thing parents who have successfully shepherded their children through divorce seem to agree on is the best adjustments are made by kids whose lives are regular, who go to bed and eat meals on time, who don't live in front of the TV set, who have well-organized activities, who have continued contact with the relatives of an absent parent as well as with the absent parent. It is also not the time to forgo discipline or to give in to every whim of a child.

Infants and Toddlers

Very young children may be unable to put a label on the experience of divorce, but even babies realize that something is different and usually react with bodily responses and regressive behavior in sleep or toilet training. When parents are anxious, toddlers sense the

Age-Appropriate Books on Divorce for Children

Many books have been written to help children at all age levels cope with the problems divorce presents for them. Many are hard to find. Most are as helpful for parents as for kids and provide starting points for talking about specific issues. A large percentage of them are intended to be read together.

If children can identify with a character or situation, it helps them interpret the events around them and sometimes provides them with an active release for their own emotions. The insights help them solve their own problems and let them move on.

Children relate to books in different ways. Don't be offended if they don't want to read about divorce or discuss "it" with you. Children may be more receptive to books and discussions six months, rather than one, after your separation.

Listed after each of the following discussions on what you can expect from your children at various ages are some books you might find helpful. Some of the titles referred to might also be found in your library. Those with an asterisk (*) before the title are available by mail from The Book Peddlers (1-800-255-3379). See page 245.

emotion and frequently become fearful themselves. The most important way you can help your infant or toddler adjust is by keeping the child's life as normal as possible. Make any necessary changes gradually. Small children react more strongly to change but also make the easiest long-term adjustment because the memory of intact family life fades faster, and new household arrangements quickly become the norm. Young children are strongly affected by day-to-day caretaking. They need reassurance, love, attention, and rituals.

Custodial mothers of young babies, particularly nursing mothers, understandably have a hard time parting with a small child. Still, it is crucial for young fathers to bond and share time with even the smallest child. This will not lessen an infant's bond to his or her mother.

- Expect your infant to cry more, to be more clingy and probably more shy than usual, perhaps even to lose his or her appetite. These are all normal reactions to a new and frightening situation over which he or she has no control.
- Realize that sleep problems, which are common anyway, are likely to surface or resurface as fears heighten.
- Treat any regression in your toddler as casually as possible. Don't encourage it; don't make a big thing of it, either. The most recent accomplishment, whether in the area of toilet training, sleeping habits, eating, or general behavior, is likely to be the first to go.
- Don't be surprised if your toddler moves rapidly from angry tantrums to apparent happiness or from withdrawn sulkiness to aggressive, reckless behavior. The insecurity a child feels as a result of change often causes swings in mood. Some children become hostile.
- Young children are likely to become increasingly irritable and cranky. They may hit siblings and behave more aggressively with other children. This, and many other expected behavior patterns, are temporary and will change over time.

What You Can Do to Help

- As early as you can, set up regular and frequent visits with your exiting spouse. Short, frequent visits if possible in the custodial home are often easier

I can't believe now that I worried only about how my two pre-teenage girls would cope with the divorce, assuming that the baby, age one, wouldn't be affected. He was confused and upset and suffered much more than the girls did.

—K. Campana, Scottsdale, AZ

on small children than moving between two residences, but children are flexible and can adapt to a commuter life-style. It's easier for a noncustodial parent to develop a personal relationship with a child on his or her own turf.

- Consider having the parent who moves out visit frequently at first, perhaps even every day for a time to participate in the bedtime routine. If visits aren't frequent, the absent parent may become a stranger to an infant or toddler.
- Provide your child with the extra needed love and attention—without smothering or spoiling your child. It is inappropriate for a child to get the attention once placed on a now-distanced spouse.
- When you need sitters, have them baby-sit your young child at your house so that the child will have as little disruption in normal routines as possible. Have your sitter keep your routines and rituals. Try to use the same sitter on a regular basis.
- Use puppets, drawings, or toys to transform information about the divorce into a story that's easier to understand.

Preschoolers

A preschooler's fear of abandonment manifests itself in various forms of separation anxiety. When parents become separated, preschoolers often fear that any negative thought they've had about a parent has come true. They think that they are now being punished for a bad wish or angry thought and are to blame for the separation. It may be useful to look at the Oedipus complex. Boys and girls at this age are often beginning their "love affairs" with parents of the opposite sex. They may have fantasized they will someday take the place of Dad in Mom's affections, or vice versa. A preschooler may unconsciously "love" the opposite-sex parent more than the same-sex parent and suddenly— to the preschooler, almost magically—the less-love parent is gone. This type of "magical thinking" can even prevent children from asking why the divorce is happening. After all, they might find out it really *is* their fault, as they suspect. Children at this age need to be told *repeatedly* that they are not being punished, and they are in no way responsible for what is happening between their parents. They need to hear that a parent leaving does not mean they are unloved or unlovable.

What You Can Do to Help

- Don't be surprised if your preschooler becomes preoccupied with "being good," especially if your separation was sudden. The child may feel that his or her former misbehavior was the cause of one parent leaving or that he or she may be sent away.
- Understand there will be added anxiety concerns when leaving the custodial parent. Review your day's schedule each morning with your child. Given a child's immature thought process, abandonment is a real fear. ("If Daddy left, might Mommy, too?") When returning to the custodial parent many children respond with a tantrum that is really an angry expression of fear and anxiety felt while that parent was away.
- Expect regression in certain areas, including perhaps a return to a forgotten security blanket or an

increase in masturbation and thumb-sucking—anything a child might think would return him or her to the safety of babyhood. Some regressive behavior, such as a loss of bowel or bladder control, will require your patience and attention. Allow regressive behavior within limits. Actually, having a security aid—a blanket or favorite toy—to fall back on can be very helpful to a child during this period.

- Be patient with a child who seems selfish. Egocentricity at this age is normal. Whether toys or parents, sharing is not an easy thing for them. ("Will I have the toys I want?") Possessiveness can also be an effort on the part of a child to regain control, to literally "hold on" to things at a time when so many events now occurring are beyond his or her control.
- Be patient with a child who becomes overly sensitive to real or imagined injuries. This may just be an expression of a need to be fussed over and cared for.
- Spend some extended one-on-one time together occasionally so that children can verbalize concerns that would otherwise go unexpressed in the rush of daily schedules.
- Don't pump a small child for stories about the other parent. You might not get the whole story and if you do, you shouldn't.

My daughter was five when she didn't let her little brother tell her noncustodial dad we had seen a movie with a male friend of mine. Later, when confronted, she said, "I didn't want Daddy to know you go to movies with other people. It would hurt his feelings." I realized what a burden my former husband and I had put on our children. I called my ex and asked him to let the children know that he goes out with friends and that he is not alone when children aren't with him. He understood, of course. It's our responsibility to take the worry out of our children's lives.
—Anna Weintraub, Los Angeles, CA

PRESCHOOL-AGE APPROPRIATE BOOKS

*THE DINOSAURS DIVORCE, by Laurene and Marc Brown (Little Brown, 1986). If dinosaurs got married, no doubt they would have to cope with divorce. Direct and lively text and comic striplike illustrations deal with various aspects of divorce, from visitation to the whys of divorce to telling friends and more.

TWO HOMES TO LIVE IN: A CHILD'S-EYE VIEW OF DIVORCE, by Barbara Hazen (Human Sciences Press, 1978). This story of a young girl whose father moves out is written in gentle and understandable prose, emphasizing that she did not cause the divorce and helping her understand her reunion fantasy, parents fighting, two Christmases, and missing her daddy.

*WHERE IS DADDY? THE STORY OF A DIVORCE, by Beth Goff (Beacon Press, 1969). This is a touching story about a little girl's confusion and fear of being abandoned when her parents divorce. Her parents fight; her dad moves out and her mom goes to work. By the end of the book, she has begun to adjust to her new life.

MOM AND DAD DON'T LIVE TOGETHER ANY MORE, by Kathy Stinson (Annick Press, 1984). Soft watercolors illustrate this little girl's description of her family's transition to joint custody parenting. It ends with her saying "My mommy and daddy love me, too. Just not together."

DIVORCE IS A GROWN-UP PROBLEM, by Janet Sinberg (Avon Books, 1978). This book shows how a child can learn to channel anger constructively and feel safe and secure because neither parent will abandon him or her. The child is actually a unisex preschooler, generic but not bland. Illustrations in black and white are suitable for coloring.

WHO WILL LEAD THE KIDDISH? by Barbara Pomerantz (UAHC, 1985). This is a story of a young Jewish girl adjusting to her parents' divorce. She spends the Shabbat at her father's apartment, where he gives her her own Kiddish cup to take home. Black and white drawings. 32 pages.

*See page 245.

Elementary School-Age Children

Children from about ages six to ten often react differently than those of other ages, sometimes suffering deeply. They're too old to use fantasy to deny the situation and too young to have the maturity or the independence to remove themselves from all the implications or realize they are not responsible. They may make excessive attempts to be compliant and submissive.

Youngsters of this age are also fearful of being displaced. (Will I have a new mother? Will there be another child taking my place in my parents' lives?) Keep in mind:

- Even when there has been poor parent-child relationship, the absent parent will be sorely missed.
- Hope for parents' reconciliation will be strong.
- Frustrated by their own sense of powerlessness, children in this age group can be intensely angry with both parents for "letting this happen."
- It's not unusual for stomachaches and headaches to occur, or for asthma to worsen.
- Watch your child's school performance, and do not hesitate to ask for a conference with the teacher if grades slip. Although some school-age children do better in school in order to shut out what's going on at home, others do poorly because they are restless and distracted with worry about their parents. Sometimes a child will let grades slip as a ploy to get both parents' attention and have them need to come together.
- Realize that your child may align him or herself with the custodial parent and try to take on an adultlike role of the absent parent. For instance, a child may try to act as a mother or father to younger siblings.

"Our children, ages nine and eleven, were angry with their father because he acted like everything was normal."
—Toni Richardson, Hopkins, MN

What You Can Do to Help

- Advise your child's teacher of the changes at home and let your child know that the teacher knows. If the school has a counselor, you may want to include that person, also.
- Enlist any and all help a school can provide if grades and behavior decline. A third party may be needed to correctly assess problems and ways to address them.
- Pay attention to your child's relationships with other children. Depression, fear of rejection, or a feeling of shame may make him or her withdraw from other kids, preferring to be with adults.
- Expect expressions of loneliness for the absent parent. Allow time for frequent visits. Remind your child how soon he or she will see the absent parent. Let your child know, too, that the absent parent misses him or her just as you do when your child is not around. Making access easier or more frequent can lessen a child's distress or longing for the departed parent. (This obviously does not apply to the absent violent or physically or sexually abusive parent.)
- Encourage contact and relationships with grandparents and other adults to ease lonely times as well as act as additional role models.
- Don't substitute food and treats for your attention. This can lead to a problem of filling "emptiness" with a poor alternative and set up a bad habit for life.

- Don't discuss financial problems with your child. Kids this age are likely to take any comments you make about having to "move to a dump," "starving," or being unable to buy "decent clothes" literally and they will begin to worry, probably without telling you.
- Both parents should give the children ample love, care, and protection.
- Be specific about pointing out that some problems are for adults only.
- Help your child to talk about the divorce with his or her friends. Because they are usually embarrassed, they often need encouragement to do so. Sleep-overs by old friends provide a natural opportunity to share this information.
- Be aware that if your child refuses to talk about the divorce, it may be because he or she is denying it or is afraid of adding to your worries. Bring up the subject and offer to answer questions at any time.

Put yourself in your child's place using words like, "*If I were seven, I think I'd be wondering about . . . Do you?*" Therapists often tell children how other children have felt about divorce. If your own parents were divorced when you were a child, or if you have observed others go through the process, tell your child how others have handled their situation.

I was touched by my seven-year-old daughter's story that she wrote about her daddy visiting her on the moon. She obviously missed him and felt he was far away. I began to encourage her father to visit and call more often.
                    —Gabrielle Peton, New Brighton, MN

ELEMENTARY SCHOOL-AGE
APPROPRIATE BOOKS

WHY ARE WE GETTING A DIVORCE? by Peter Mayle (Crown, 1978/88). With a blend of humor, sensitivity, and fun illustrations, this book covers many difficult issues with objectivity. Topics discussed with sympathy and reassurance are: why people marry, divorce misconceptions, adjusting to living with one parent, as well as dealing with feelings of loss and hurt.

THE DIVORCE WORKBOOK: A GUIDE FOR KIDS AND FAMILIES, by Ives, Fassler & Lash (Waterfront Books, Burlington, VT 05401). Interactive book to help children sort out feelings.

I WISH I HAD MY FATHER, by Norma Simon (Albert Whitman, 1983). For children who struggle with the feelings of rejection and sadness caused by a parent who has left them.

PLEASE COME HOME, by Doris Sanford (Multnomeh Press, Portland, Oregon, 1985). Lovely color illustrations about an 8-year-old girl who wonders what will happen to her now that Daddy has gone. Her teddy bear comforts her, but she learns to feel okay by herself. "I used to think I'd hurt forever but I don't."

MEGAN'S BOOK OF DIVORCE, by Erica Jong (New American Library, 1984). Precocious 4-year-old Megan tells her side of the story of her parents' separation and her enlightened joint-custody situation. Each parent has a "significant other." In the end, she admits that divorce isn't so bad, because there's no more fighting and she has four grown-ups to hug her and twice as many birthday presents.

TWO PLACES TO SLEEP, by Joan Schuchman (Carolrhoda Books, 1979). Nice drawings by Jim LaMarche illustrate the story of 7-year-old David, who lives with his father in their original house and visits his mother in her apartment on weekends. It emphasizes his happiness with each parent and that he is loved as much as ever and that the divorce is not his fault.

AT DADDY'S ON SATURDAYS, by Linda Girard (Albert Whitman, 1988). After Katie's parents divorce, her daddy moves away. Saturdays seem far away but her mother and her teacher help her through the week until Saturday, when she does see her father.

Preteens and Teenagers

Preteens and adolescents aren't necessarily better equipped to deal with divorce because of their age. Anger and uncertainty are normal reactions for these kids, although they may be more adept at hiding these feelings. Teenagers sometimes find it easier to express their anger and sadness.

Adolescents' needs are different from those of younger children. They are learning to separate from the family as a unit in their growth toward independence. Divorce poses additional conflicts for them in this area. They often feel the need to align themselves with one parent and become more attached to the idea of upholding the family unit. Others take the opportunity to "slip between the cracks," and separate all too effectively from the family, avoiding any parental discipline or responsibility.

If a household is tense and family fights are frequent, a teen's basic reaction will simply be to escape. Escape can take many forms, including detachment, staying away from the house, drug use, leaving school, and even choosing an unwanted pregnancy in order to feel needed and be loved.

In spite of their normal rebelliousness, teens are likely to be very moralistic and judgmental about divorce. They tend to make a scapegoat of the parent they think is to blame. They're vulnerable to being used unfairly as an ally by one parent against the other. They will have a hard time slotting the departing parent as a good person. They will also believe that parents are very selfish to disrupt their lives this way. It's important to remember that:

- Although your adolescent may *seem* better able to cope with your divorce than younger children in the family, he or she may very well be feeling a great deal of pain and embarrassment.
- Teens may experience fears that their own marriages may fail someday and question marriage for themselves; others will say, "I'm never going to have children and put them through this."
- If a daughter blames her mother for her father's departure (if he left for another woman), she may be feeling rejected herself and may need some counseling so as not to carry this into her own future relationships with men.
- Teens are usually upset and embarrassed with their parents' sexual needs. It's also difficult for them to deal with their parents' sexuality while in the process of learning about their own. Sometimes there is actual competition with parents in this area.
- Even articulate teenagers who have previously been good communicators may withdraw temporarily as their way of dealing with their feelings. They may fear hurting a parent's feelings and keep their pain to themselves.
- A teen who sides with the parent who does not initiate a divorce may be responding to a need to balance out the family scenario by providing companionship and emotional support to a parent perceived as the one deserted.
- Some teens choose healthy escape by spending more time with a friend or relative. It's hard not to see this as rejection of a parent, but it is usually just a temporary response by the child.

What You Can Do to Help

- Practice (or learn) good communication skills. Sentences should start with "I feel (concerned, confused, sad, unhappy) ... when ..." rather than "You are (late, sloppy, wrong) ..."
- Assure your kids that although the divorce may feel embarrassing, it is not shameful. You are still a family ... yes, in a different configuration ... and there are still two parents who care for and about them. Just verbalizing the word *embarrassing* will define their feelings so they can begin to deal with them.
- Encourage your child to continue developing his or her independence and outside circle of interests: school, athletics, friends. If you are the noncustodial parent, be prepared to provide transportation and/or attend school activities and sports events, so your child won't have to give them up in order to see you.
- Make as much time as you can for attending school conferences, performances, or athletic events in which your child participates. Teenagers need you to show your interest as much as preschoolers.
- Give teens as much information as they ask for and can handle. They often look for simplistic answers and may draw inaccurate and unfair conclusions. Some may adopt a pseudo-mature attitude and try to become more involved than they should be in marital issues.
- Don't forgo setting reasonable limits, rules, and curfews for a teen. Many teens need more structure rather than less in times of turmoil. Excuse the verbal attacks you may have to tolerate, but be cautious about giving in too much.
- Remember, there is a big difference between babysitting a neighbor's child and looking after a younger

sibling. Teens will resent responsibilities dumped
on them unless they are part of a discussion and
decision-making process.
- Be careful not to turn to your preteen or teenager
for more support, assistance, or companionship than
he or she can give, at that age. Some kids rise to the
occasion and enjoy increased self-esteem, but others find themselves resentful of the extra demands
and confused about how they should handle an
unfamiliar role. Let their behavior and words be
your guide.
- Don't pump teens for information about the other
parent, or encourage them to take sides. It will
make them feel manipulated, coerced, or bribed.
- Watch for signs of trouble, ranging from denial and
depression to running away, suicidal threats, or
drug use. If you discover your teen is showing signs
of any kind of chemical abuse, get professional help
at once.
- Think back to your own feelings during adolescence and stretch your tolerance and level of
understanding.

Custody for teens can be more complicated than for
younger children, because they may have their own
preferences that will have to be taken into account. An
older teen can scarcely be forced to live with a parent
he or she refuses to tolerate. A discussion of the pros
and cons of living with either parent may be necessary.
For a child leaving for boarding school or college,
this time is especially complicated. Such a child needs
reassurance that each parent will stay in touch and
will visit. A departing teen is dealing with his or her
own feelings of separation and isolation. You will also
have to determine where and with whom the holidays
will be spent. Changing the place where a child feels

"based" during that first year away can add significantly to the stress that child will experience.

Your child has, most likely, spent his or her life
relating to parents as a unit. Now, as your maturing
teen learns to relate to each parent as a separate and
unique person, you can expect and look forward to the
development of new and sometimes better relationships.

When I worked at Domestic Relations Court, I often talked
with teenagers who had lived with one parent since the
divorce and now wanted a chance to get to know the
other parent. It wasn't that they no longer loved that
parent or that the living arrangements were no longer
suitable. However, as they spent more time discovering
who they were, they needed to know more about who
their "noncustodial parent" was. Sometimes they would
spend a few months, a year, maybe just a few weeks there
and then be satisfied. They would then ask to move back.
People sometimes said, "Children shouldn't be allowed
to play one parent against the other so much," but I saw
it as a normal response.

—Sally Brush, Aring Institute, Cincinnati, OH

PRETEEN- AND
TEENAGE-APPROPRIATE BOOKS

*HOW IT FEELS WHEN PARENTS DIVORCE, by Jill
Krementz (Knopf, 1984). In this moving book, beauti-
fully illustrated with the author's photographs, twenty
girls and boys from 7 to 16 express their feelings about
their parents' divorces. They talk honestly about their
feelings, the good and bad parts of joint custody, and
the adjustments they must make when their parents
begin to date or remarry. Young readers will be reas-
sured that they are not alone. Parents will also gain
insight into their children's feelings.

THE KIDS' BOOK OF DIVORCE: BY, FOR AND ABOUT KIDS, by Eric E. Rofes, ed. (Random House, 1981). Twenty kids from 11 to 14 discuss parents who were divorced, and their fears about divorce. The children split up into small groups to write the chapters. The editor suggests that parents and children read the book together, because many parts are springboards for discussion.

THE KIDS' GUIDE TO DIVORCE, by J. Brogan and U. Maiden (Fawcett, 1986). An easy, conversational book that discusses the practical issues that affect children. Offers an end-of-book questionnaire so kids can compare their answers with others who have taken it.

WHAT'S GOING TO HAPPEN TO ME?, by Edna LeShan (Macmillan, 1978). For children 9 and older. This book discusses joint custody, value of family therapy, and how to retain a belief in marriage.

*IT'S NOT THE END OF THE WORLD, by Judy Blume (Dell, 1972). The ever-popular Judy Blume tackles the problems of divorce through the eyes of a 12-year-old girl, the middle child of three. She takes on the impossible task of getting her separated parents back together again; her older brother runs away; and her little sister becomes sad and withdrawn. Once the divorce is accomplished and the fighting stops, the children settle down, realizing that life's not all bad.

THE DIVORCE EXPRESS, by Paula Danzier (Delacorte, 1982). In this humorous novel about a joint custody family, Phoebe spends weekdays with her father in the suburbs and commutes back to the city to be with her mother for weekends on a bus called the "divorce express."

*See page 245.

YOUR CHILD AS YOUR PEER

Beware of the stressful family syndrome of making your child your confidante and companion, which family therapists report occurring with increasing frequency among single parents. It seems so right and so easy to devote yourself to your child, but boundaries of adult-child roles become blurred. Using a child as a crutch delays many parents from getting out and building new lives for themselves. The old-fashioned idea that certain information ranging from financial worries to details about adult relationships is not for "children's ears" has faded. But the parent acting as a peer puts an unhealthy responsibility on a child's shoulders. Being in on everything may give a child a temporary feeling of importance, but children who are "parentified" give up part of their childhood, and therapists are now hearing about it. A child can feel responsible for a parent's happiness and may feel reluctant (and guilty) about moving out on his or her own. So:

- Don't confide in your child about your sexual involvements, the financial details of your life, or your general unhappiness with life.
- Beware of turning a formerly marriage-centered home into a child-centered home.
- Don't mistake your child's understanding and sensitivity to your needs for a reason to turn him or her into a sounding board; seek out group or individual therapy if you need someone to talk to.
- Don't confuse being your child's best friend with your child being your best friend. Children benefit from a strong parent who can listen and be available.

A child who has been like a best friend for years may make a dramatic break with you when he or she

becomes a teenager. Sometimes, the tighter the parent/
child bond in younger years, the more dramatic the
break may be as that growing-up child asserts a sense
of self. As parents, we must learn to "let go" so our
children are not forced to make divisive breaks themselves; this is especially important for families in which
parents think, "It's you and me against the world, kid."

---

*The worst aspect of being pals with your child is you lose
your authority. Sometimes you compromise what you
think is right when you try to be a pal to your kid.*
                                —Linda Lich, Lake Odessa, MI

GENDER-RELATED CONCERNS

One of the most significant variables, according to
the research conducted by Dr. John Guidubaldi of Kent
State University, is that of gender. Girls consistently
demonstrated better adjustment than boys in divorced
households, ranging from social skills to school grades.
In fact, says Guidubaldi ". . . the divorce of their parents hardly seemed to affect them."

Young boys, it appears, take divorce observably harder
than girls—perhaps because it's usually the father who
leaves home. They may have difficulties with friends
and teachers at school because they are more likely
than girls to act out their anger and tend to be more
aggressive and physical, in general. Guidubaldi's study
indicated that boys will do just as well as others in
school if they are in contact with the noncustodial
male parent. Interestingly, studies show that boys in
joint custody were significantly better adjusted than
boys in sole maternal custody.

A 1988 study by Sheila Krein at the University of Illinois–Urbana indicates that boys, even more than girls, in single-parent homes are likely to get less education than other kids by completing 1.7 fewer years in school.

Girls' gender-related problems often catch up with them during adolescence, when they need to know they are important to the opposite sex. Sometimes a girl will think a father might have left because there is something wrong with her. Actually, the opposite-sex parent of both a son or a daughter makes a major contribution to a child's confidence in his or her appeal to the opposite sex and in attitudes toward men and women as their children mature. As pointed out in the October 1985 issue of *Family Relations*, there is little support for the popular myth that parental absence after divorce produces either effeminate sons, promiscuous daughters, or juvenile delinquents. In fact, studies show that divorce is an unreliable predictor of mental illness, low achievement, or delinquency in children and adolescents.

All things being equal, children seem to do better with the same-sex parent. In other words, boys living with their fathers and girls living with their mothers are often better adjusted. Boys who live with their mothers may suffer for the absence of male role models. Don't be too quick to assume there are no other accessible male role models around. A male teacher, a grandfather, a favorite uncle, a caring older cousin, or a neighborhood friend may well serve as a model and have long-term positive effects on a boy. A well-screened high school or college male baby-sitter can fill the role of big brother, too. TV and movies also influence children in positive ways.

Gay Parents and Gender Concerns

Though divorce based on one parent's orientation for a same-sex partner has become less of a closet issue, it still adds additional complications and considerations to an already difficult life change. Children and the adult left in the marriage may have additional adjustments because society has not yet totally accepted the gay and lesbian life-style. Both adults and children will need to learn how to separate feelings toward the gay parent from the gay parent's sexual orientation.

Professional counseling is usually very helpful in this situation. It can be advantageous to find someone who is sensitive to this issue. Still, the painful issues of breaking up a marriage are the same for the heterosexual or homosexual alike. You may be lucky to find in one counselor help with dealing with the sexual issues as well as the separation issues, or you might need to find two.

Children do need honest answers. Most children are—and should be—told about the gay parent by the gay parent. Children who are old enough to understand its implications will have many questions, some verbalized, some not. For instance, "Does this mean I will be gay? If I tell my friends, will they think I'm gay? Do I have to keep this a secret? Who can I trust enough to tell this to? Will anyone want to date me?"

Children of all ages need to know that they are no more likely to be gay than children by two heterosexual parents. Older children will need help in dealing with their own embarrassment. Adolescents are sensitive to anything out of the ordinary when it comes to their parents, including the delicate issue of sexuality. They need to hear that their family is still acceptable, albeit different from those of most of their peers. Adjustment will be easiest for children when, as in every other divorce, parents can deal with them in a cooperative fashion while working out their own relationship outside the parenting arena.

Though state and county statutes and specific judges may influence the outcome, a custody case should not be expected to be lost based on a parent's sexuality; it is advisable, however, to keep this issue out of the divorce process. Being frank about one parent's sexuality may well jeopardize chances for joint custody, regardless of how agreeable you and your spouse may be about it.

Gay parents can be good parents, or less than adequate parents—just like everyone else. The desire to have and/or live with one's children is separate from one's sexuality. And there are many gay parents. One out of ten gay men are fathers; one out of three lesbians are mothers. Eighty-seven percent of the children of a gay parent were born in the framework of a heterosexual marriage. Many cities are now offering parenting and support groups to gay and lesbian parents and their children as they cope with the additional unique concerns of their life-styles.

GAY PARENT SUPPORT

WHOSE CHILD CRIES? Children of Gay Parents Talk About Their Lives, by Joe Gantz (Jalmar Press, 1983).

GAY PARENTING: A Complete Guide for Gay Men and Lesbians with Children, by Joy Schulenburg (Doubleday Anchor, 1985).

Lesbian Rights Project, 1370 Mission St., San Francisco, CA 94102, (415) 621-0674 provides free legal advice and counseling when men or women are discriminated against on the basis of sexual orientation. They also make available materials and books.

ADULT CHILDREN CAN STILL BE CHILDLIKE

Divorcing couples expect adult children to be minimally disturbed, because these children no longer need their parents' care and have their own interests. This is not necessarily so. Reactions of adult children are often similar to those of younger ones, but on a different level. They may mourn a lost way of life, feeling that their cherished memories of family life are only illusions. They may be embarrassed, especially if a parent is involved with a younger person, perhaps someone their own age. And they may be angry at being burdened with what they feel is another problem—their parents' need for emotional support—at a time when they have problems of their own. The following advice may be helpful:

- Do not tell your adult children that you stayed together for their sake, whether or not that's true. They may be resentful.
- Help them understand that "all those years" were not a sham, that it's okay to keep their warm memories intact. Remind them that people change and that parents are people, not statues on pedestals.
- Be prepared to see these young adults take sides just as younger children sometimes do. They often feel protective of the parent who they think is the "victim." Even as adults they need to have permission to be with both parents. After six months or so their initial anger will lessen as they try to establish new relationships with each parent.
- Take advantage of the opportunities you now have as an individual to build new relationships with your children. You no longer have to relate to them as a parenting team.
- Don't insist that grown children come home to spend holidays with you if they seem reluctant. Some

young people find it difficult to return when there's no longer a "real family" and the old traditions cannot be continued. If they have their own families, it is important for them to establish their own traditions in their own homes. You may want to visit them during vacations and long weekends.

SIBLING SUPPORT

Little has been written about siblings as support for each other during divorce. Although it has been suggested that divorce is harder for an only child, this perhaps has more to do with the fact that when one parent moves out, a larger "percentage" of that family has diminished than when there are two or more children. Sibling support seems to come more from the presence of sharing an experience than from talking about it. In fact, children seem to discuss it very little with each other and don't know how to use each other as a resource or for emotional support. Lack of experience about "feeling" talk is one suggested reason. When exposed to other children in a group situation, however, children begin to learn how to put words to feelings that can help relieve the anger and stress being experienced. Also, be aware that children will be more prone to discussing their parents and the divorce with a sibling if they disagree with the other sibling's different attitude or perception of one parent's behavior. This lends more to personal judgments and division rather than to help and support.

One study on twins has indicated that fathers who remain active in the lives of their twin children after separation lessen "twinning behavior" (twin dependency, shyness, passivity), particularly with male twins. An active father helps them develop as individuals.

> *Our kids were fighting a lot and wanted each parent to each have one of them separately at each house in our joint custody situation and switch "them" each week. They said, "If you and Daddy can get a divorce, why can't we?" While I was willing to do it now and then, my basic response was "NO!"*
>
> —Julie Hall, Boca Raton, FL

WHEN PROFESSIONAL HELP IS CALLED FOR

Although some children make it through their parents' separation and divorce fairly easily, others feel the aftershocks of a divorce months and even years later, suffering socially, academically, and emotionally. One researcher found that half of a group of preschoolers were more troubled a year after their parents' divorces than they had been immediately after. In most cases, these were children whose parents were still feeling hurt and rage and were not supplying consistent care for them. Even though it's not reasonable to wait five years to seek professional help, it is worthwhile to give your child some time to adjust, perhaps six months or a year, if problems aren't severe.

Above all, remind yourself that not every behavorial and emotional problem any child displays is a direct result of divorce. One fight at school or one bedwetting incident doesn't have to be related to the divorce. Many will be normal developmental occurrences common to children in any home. Books that trace the development of children through the grade-school years are excellent resources for understanding normal versus problematic behavior.

But repeated problems in any one area or lower

school performance should be addressed. Difficult behavior doesn't mean a child is psychologically disturbed. Children need time—and sometimes extra outside help—to adjust. Discipline is usually the key family issue that prompts a family to seek professional help. Discipline problems can arise from children's inability to sort out feelings or adjust to the separation. Or a child may just lack good coping skills. Misbehavior can be the result of fear, hostility, or insecurity and a signal that the child needs more positive attention for himself. Children who are unsuccessful at obtaining enough positive "strokes" will try to get any kind, including negative ones. "Misbehaving" at least gets a parent's attention, and children prefer that to being ignored.

Long-term studies show that only 30 percent of the people going through divorce have serious social adjustment problems—the same percentage for the population in general. This is not meant to dismiss the fact that this transitional time creates real emotional trauma but rather to help you keep long-term problems in perspective. You can't always make children happy, or speed up their grief process. Your children will eventually have to adjust to the reality of divorce by themselves. Near the end of the first year, they should have:

- Accepted the reality that the family will not be living together anymore, and that you will not return to the other parent. (Most kids never quite give up fantasies that you will reunite, but this fact should be set aside, at least intellectually.)
- Separated themselves from your adult conflicts and returned to their normal absorption with themselves and their own activities. If you've moved, they should have adjusted to a new home and new school and new friends.

- Stopped blaming themselves for your breakup.
- Developed the self-confidence that allows them to speak up if they feel one parent (or both) is using him or her as a messenger.
- Learned to refuse to allow one parent to "bad-mouth" the other.

Hopefully it will only take a year for children to come to terms with their basic feelings of loss of the original family and any rejection or desertion by a parent, although some anger and sadness may still persist. It's comforting to know that if they have made a successful adjustment, your children will have learned invaluable skills that they'll use later in life.

RESENTMENT HURTS MOST THE ONE WHO FEELS IT.

When Counseling Will Help

Children whose parents fight a lot and then divorce seem to need more help than children whose parents fight a little and then divorce. As we have said, children are most affected by parents' angry behavior.

Although you can't get inside your kids' heads and speed up the grieving or get rid of the anger, you *can* try to provide professional help. There are many avenues of help to explore. Short-term counseling has proven to be effective for children and families. Don't let tight finances prevent you from seeking professional help. Some services are free or available on a sliding-scale fee. But do make sure the counselor is experienced in handling family problems.

Places to turn to are:

- *Public schools.* They often offer short-term counseling groups for children during or after school hours.

- *Your employer's health coverage.* Your plan may include family counseling. If your children are also covered on your ex's insurance, check for the best coverage.
- *Family service agencies.* Social service agencies, or local chapters of the United Way often offer special parenting and divorce groups.
- Local hotlines, divorce counseling groups, or a woman's center.
- Recommendations made by your personal physician, the local county medical association, or American Psychiatric Association.
- Marriage and family counselors listed in the Yellow Pages. (Or write to: The American Association of Marriage and Family Therapy, 924 West 9th St., Upland, CA 91786.)

Consider Professional Help When:

- Your child has shown uncharacteristically poor school performance for a semester or so, even after you've consulted and worked on the problems with teachers and school counselors.
- Your child is losing friends because he or she is unusually aggressive or apathetic and cannot seem to get along with anyone.
- Your child shows uncharacteristically intense anger and throws many tantrums or overreacts to minor situations.
- Your child has had prolonged mood swings that range from hostility to extreme affection.
- Your child continues to grieve unrestrainedly for the absent parent or the former family life.
- You see other radical changes in your child's behavior, such as continuous problems in school, cheating, lying, or stealing, use of alcohol or other drugs.

Most parents wait until there is a crisis or major problem before seeking professional help. Be open to counseling before a major crisis occurs. You needn't wait for a long and obvious list of problems and concerns to develop, either. Use your judgment and your knowledge of your child and trust your comfort level and parental intuition. It may be only one event that your child can't share with either parent that may trigger a need for a counselor to help the family; other times unusual behavior can be a deep-rooted cry for help.

Besides addressing particular issues, therapists can also work to repair a child's self-esteem and provide him or her with better coping skills. Therapy can validate feelings of frustration, reduce stress, and help give children a new sense of control. Keep in mind that therapy often requires the presence of all or various family members along the way to be effective. Getting counseling for a child should not mean scapegoating, or trying to identify the child as "the one with the problem."

Some therapists use "play therapy" not only to treat symptoms but to prevent problems with younger children. By moving around toys or figures that represent family members and talking about these relationships, professionals can often prevent concerns from becoming concrete problems later in life.

Some unresolved emotional problems show up as physical symptoms rather than behavior problems. Medical attention will be needed for the symptoms, but counseling may be required as well for the emotional cause.

Above all, children need to know that feelings of sadness, anger, guilt, and fear don't mean they themselves are bad, unlovable, or crazy. They need to know they can "love Daddy" even though Mommy doesn't. Sometimes these words must come from a neutral third party, despite the fact that they've gotten words of reassurance from a parent. A third party can also help family communications to take place safely among family members.

My nine-year-old son was waking up grouchy almost every day. He never wanted to try anything new or different. I didn't realize he needed professional help until we had our pictures taken at a portrait studio. The proofs showed that he was in pain and uncomfortable, stilted and not smiling real easily. He's seeing a therapist now and one year later is my own happy-go-lucky son again.
— Andrea Posgay, Minnetonka, MN

If YOU are unable to cope with daily routines in your job, or social life, seek professional help—especially if you are abusing yourself or your children with drugs, alcohol, or through neglect. Getting help if you are unable to cope is the greatest gift you can give your children. These same resources that prove helpful with them are available to you. Seeking appropriate help for you and your children is both an act of love—and a sign of strength.

If You Have Lost Control

Physical abuse of your children is not okay. If you find yourself on the verge of striking a child, or your temper escalates more than usual, remember that this divorce is affecting you, too. It may be time for you to get some help for yourself. You'll need help in learning how to cope constructively with your anger and frustration. You owe it to your children. Get help from private counseling or contact: Parents Anonymous, 233 Hawthorne Blvd. #208, Torrance, CA 90505, 1-800-352-0386.

There are chapters in each state with weekly meeting and no dues. Each state has a 24-hour hotline.

DON'T SPEND TIME REGRETTING THE THINGS YOU'VE DONE —RATHER THE THINGS YOU HAVEN'T DONE.

BUILDING OR REBUILDING A KID'S SELF-ESTEEM

In the pain and confusion of separation and divorce, we all tend to feel lost and unloved, children especially so. Our good feelings about ourselves often seem like they've turned to sand running through our punctured egos. Children don't know that there will be enough love to go around once their parents live apart. Prove them wrong! And, parents sometimes feel (unconsciously) that there isn't enough love available to them from their children if the kids have to share it in two households. Wrong again! Following are some good ideas to get everyone back on track.

- Show your children a lighted candle and indicate that the flame represents your love. Then light another candle off of that flame to represent the other parent's love. Neither is diminished. A third candle can be lit from either of these two flames. Again, neither flame is diminished. Moral: There is plenty of love to go around.
- The "love bucket" metaphor is a good one to share with every child to help learn how to ask for extra loving. Each of us carries a love bucket. Sometimes, as we carry it around, it can get low from sloshing over the top, from evaporation, or from an occasional spill. Everyone's love bucket needs refilling from time to time, but because we can't actually see when the other person's bucket is low, we must tell someone else so they can help us get it refilled.

A CHILD'S BILL OF RIGHTS

I. The right of the child to be treated as an interested and affected person and not as a pawn.

II. The right to grow up in the home environment that will best guarantee an opportunity to achieve mature and responsible citizenship.

III. The right to the day-by-day love, care, discipline, and protection of the custodial parent.

IV. The right to know the noncustodial or each parent having joint custody and to have the benefit of such parent's love and guidance through adequate visitation.

V. The right to a positive and constructive relationship with both parents, with neither parent permitted to degrade the other in the child's mind.

VI. The right to have moral and ethical values inculcated by precept and example, and to have limits set for behavior so that the child may develop self-discipline early in life.

VII. The right to the most adequate level of economic support that can be provided by the efforts of both parents.

VIII. The right to the same opportunities for education that the child would have had if the family unit had not been transformed.

IX. The right to such periodic review of custodial arrangements and child-support orders as the parents' circumstances and the child's benefit require.

X. The right to the recognition of the fact that children involved in a divorce are always disadvantaged parties, and the law must take affirmative steps to assure their welfare.

Adopted from Wisconsin Supreme Court decisions

Please photocopy these tips and share them with your children.

TIPS FOR CHILDREN*

(HOW TO SURVIVE YOUR PARENTS' FIGHTS)

First, understand IT IS NOT YOUR FAULT. Parents' arguments, like decisions about divorce or separation, are their business and not kids' fault or responsibility. Don't feel guilty when your parents argue. It is not up to you to get them to stop.

Second, DON'T TRY TO SOLVE YOUR PARENTS' PROBLEMS. Only they can do that. If you try, you will probably get caught in the middle, and that will only make matters worse. Don't take sides. If one parent asks your opinion or advice or in other ways tries to pull you into the middle of a disagreement, just say, "I think I'd better stay out of this."

Third, LEAVE THE ROOM WHEN YOUR PARENTS ARGUE. Find some activity that helps take your mind off of it. Call a friend, put on a favorite record or video, take up your hobby in the basement.

Fourth, KNOW THAT THESE EXPERIENCES ARE REALLY HARD ON EVERYONE. It's not easy to live through such confusing times. You're not crazy to feel the way you do. Remember, arguing may be scary, but it isn't the end of the world. An argument can be an effective way of working out a disagreement.

Fifth, DON'T KEEP YOUR FEELINGS IN-SIDE. Find someone you can trust, talk to them. This may be a parent. It could be a grandparent, friend, teacher, clergy, counselor, or older brother or sister.

Ask your parents for what you need, such as:

- Please spend some time *alone* with me, even five minutes of my very own time, not related to school, room cleaning, or things like that.

- Even if you are sure my "other" parent will hurt me, please let me learn myself. I'd like you there with a hug if I do get hurt . . . and please don't say "I told you so!"

- Please don't call me the man or mother of the house. I NEED TO BE A CHILD.

- Please trust me if, once in a while, I don't want to talk. Sometimes, even though you are ready, I'm not.

- Don't react with anger when I say I want to live with the other parent. Usually when I say it, I am angry, hurt, and scared, too.

- Please let me tell you what I want to tell you about my visits with the other parent. Often I'm afraid I'll hurt your feelings if I tell you that I had a good time.

*Source: The Aring Institute, 6881 Beechmont Avenue, Cincinnati, OH 45230, (513)231-6630.

Ideas for Rebuilding a Kid's Self-esteem

• Conscious use of verbal praise is obvious, but it works. Better yet, praise "overheard," such as that spoken on the phone or to another, is a good technique.

• Letting a child be in charge can help overcome feelings of helplessness. Cooking in the kitchen and making some of the daily decisions are just two ways to implement this idea.

• Do little things to let your children know you love them, from leaving notes in their lunch boxes to a little surprise on their pillow at night. (To add to your repertoire of ideas, see my book *101 Ways to Tell Your Child "I Love You"* (Contemporary Books, 1988).

3

"D"-Day: Departure Day

If you are approaching "D"-Day, knowing that it will be difficult, knowing the questions to ask yourself and being as prepared as possible will make it easier for you. If it is behind you, then you have made it past a milestone and are moving on. For many, this is the hardest day you will have to get through. Discussed by few, it is remembered by all touched by it.

From a child's point of view, a divorce does not begin until one parent moves out. As strange as it may seem, letting your children share apartment-hunting with the departing parent can actually be a very helpful preparation for "D"-Day. Custodial parents should not make comments on the size or cost of the abode the departing parent will occupy. Try not to be hurt by the children's excitement or enjoyment of finding a new living space with their other parent. It reaffirms the departing parent's words that the children will participate in his or her life and new home as well as showing that this parent will continue to participate in the children's lives.

PREPARATION FOR "D"-DAY

Assuming that the departing spouse's move is set for a definite date, you can plan the activities of the day. The custodial parent should be sure to schedule something interesting if he or she will be alone, perhaps plan something there's never been enough time for—a massage, lunch with friends, whatever.

Most custodial parents hang around the house until the move is complete. You may still wonder about protocol. Do you help your spouse pack? Do one last load of laundry? Or do you hide in the guest room? Older children may wish to go with the parent who is leaving to help him or her set up the new household. Others may find it too painful to help a parent move out of the house. There really aren't any answers to these questions. Each family handles them differently.

I moved out on Father's Day. Talk about bad timing!
—*Rod Martel, Minneapolis, MN*

Laying Your Plans

- Set the time for the departure as early in the day as possible. If it's scheduled for afternoon or evening, everyone will be nervous and apprehensive for the entire day.
- Let the children know the whens, wheres, and hows of the move.
- Let children who will remain at home have a voice in deciding how the day will be spent. It will probably be better for them to be with a parent, instead of going off to visit friends, but if they're old enough to have definite preferences, let them choose. (This day may be the first of many during which you do your child a favor by not making him or her responsible for providing companionship for you.)

The girls were going with my husband to help him settle into the apartment, so I had the whole day alone. I got up very early and stood in the rain for an hour in order to be among the first admitted to an estate sale. The wait was worthwhile; I bought a beautiful chest to replace one my husband was taking with him and a few lamps and other things I could never have found anywhere else. When I got home, my brother came over to help me move into another bedroom. I'd always loved the view from the upstairs guest room, and now that's all mine.
—*K. Campana, Scottsdale, AZ*

Don't strive to keep the day "normal" by following every accustomed routine; let it be different. Eat dinner earlier or later than usual, perhaps in a different room (at least be sure to remove the vacant chair!); spend the evening doing something unusual. Consider letting a sad and worried child sleep with you or just camp out in a sleeping bag in your bedroom.

Have the kids help Daddy get his stuff together. It gives the kids a feeling of participation and can turn a really unpleasant occasion into an almost celebratory event!
—*Hester Mundis, W. Shokan, NY*

Splitting Up the Household Goods

Parents take for granted that the furniture in the house belongs to them. Certain items have personal, premarital claims—the bedroom set that came from one's own childhood room, for example, or the chair inherited from one's aunt. Those are the easy items to divide. The things that are hard to make decisions about, hard for everyone to agree upon (as you'll realize when you hear the kids voicing their opinions), are those bought to complete the furnishing of the house for use by the whole family. If the departure takes place with short notice (or none at all) with one spouse moving into furnished quarters, a selection of kitchen-ware may be all that may go initially. Ideally, if the departing spouse must furnish an apartment or a house, he or she can decide in a first-round discussion what will be taken and will take just that. Bear in mind, though, that repeated trips to pick up furniture make children feel that their home is being stripped and dismantled. Except for personal items, everything in the house is viewed by children as theirs! It is their home. They may regard the removal of anything as the very dismantling of their *lives*. That doesn't mean that furniture and possessions shouldn't be moved, but awareness of their feelings may influence your actions and feelings.

If the departing spouse's new apartment or house is not being planned as a "second home" for the children, or if it will be far away and rarely visited, the fewer possessions removed the better. But if the departing spouse decides that he or she is actually setting up an alternative place for the children to live part of the time, it's best for the remaining parent to adopt that same philosophy and share possessions. This may be difficult, considering the stress and anger—or even hate—of the moment, but:

- Do *not* put off any decision about division of possessions until the last minute. Make the easiest ones first, then move on to the others in order of their difficulty. Ideally, you should tour the house and discuss what will go several days or a week before the move.
- If you are actually dividing the household possessions in half, consider adopting the time-honored

method of taking turns when you make choices about your possessions.

- Not every item needs to be dealt with at this time; some items will be settled with the divorce decree or legal separation agreement. Once you are settled in your new place, household items may seem more or less important. Remember, nothing is final until the divorce is.
- The intrinsic value of many items may be more important than monetary worth. Family photos can be duplicated, even if only by photocopying.
- Taking some of the children's belongings to the "other" residence may be difficult for the parent at home, but it is real evidence of the out-of-house parent's willingness to create a space and a place for his or her children. Taking furniture, toys, or clothes should first be discussed with your children.
- Be prepared to compromise and to let your children see that you do actually live by your often-expressed belief that there are more important things in life than material goods.

Maybe living together was costly emotionally, but setting up two households is costly, too. The money it takes to set up a second home comes out of marital assets. Be prepared for feelings you never anticipated, from being jealous of your exiting spouse's new furniture to resentment at leaving the family homestead that you didn't think was important to you.

Many exiting spouses find themselves moving in with their parents temporarily while they deal with the expense of the divorce and while they figure out where they'll go and what they'll do. This delays the process of setting up a new home for themselves and the children, as well as putting extra emotional stresses on parenting roles and creating conflicts about who is in charge.

POST-"PARTING" DEPRESSION

It's not surprising that most people feel post-separation depression. In even the most well-managed and amicable of situations, parents should expect to endure a "recovery period" for both themselves and their children. What's important to remember is that life will go on, things will get better, and a satisfying family life can be attained.

CHILDREN NEVER LOSE A MOTHER OR
FATHER WHO OPTS TO STAY ACTIVE
IN THEIR LIVES, THOUGH EVERY
PARENT HAS THIS INITIAL FEAR.

Children need to be able to look back on their childhood with a history of both parents active in their lives. After all, *you never are replaced by anyone else as mother or father in your children's lives,* even if the other parent remarries or paints a terrible picture of you to your children.

It's not possible to predict what range of emotions you may feel at this time. It is different for each person. But for every person it is intense. What's also amazing is the either/or range of feelings that can exist side by side. Relief and pain, laughter and tears can all occur simultaneously. The physical side of your emotions may be a surprise. And it is physiological. Sadness, anger, and pain never *felt* this way before. You may feel exhausted and periodically immobilized.

When the Door Closes from the Inside

Once your soon-to-be-ex-spouse has left:

- Allow yourself and the children to cry, to grieve, if you feel sad. Don't shut yourself off from the kids or try to "protect" them by not letting them share feelings with you.

- Then do something—preferably something active. Rearrange the furniture if your spouse's move has left gaps, straighten closets and cupboards, clean the house. Involve the children by going out. Do something physical—bike, bowl, swim, or just have a running race.

- Begin immediately to show the willingness to accept a new way of life and the determination that will make things get better, for both you and the children. Most kids of any age will take their cues from your attitude; if you can handle this, they can. If you can't, get help; the children will pick up on your worries.

- Vent anger now (or later) by using acceptable ways to let off steam. Create a punching bag out of a laundry bag; slam a pillow with a tennis racket; dig in the garden; find an out-of-the-way room or closet or place where you can shout out epithets at the top of your lungs. Tear up magazines or newspaper, wad them into balls, and have a good paper fight. Chop wood, hammer nails, swim! Get physical!

- Write down your sad feelings—or your anger—if you prefer a quieter expressive vehicle.

- Consider planning a physical activity for the last part of the day, especially after the door closes for the last time. Healthful and tiring exercise such as skiing, biking, swimming, or bowling will provide opportunities to work off feelings of sadness, anger, and depression.

I found that if I talked about my feelings, it gave my kids permission to talk about their feelings. Also helpful was the opening line, "You're having feelings, aren't you?" Then we'd go from there.

—Kate Green, St. Paul, MN

When the Door Closes from the Outside

If you are the departing spouse, the changes in your life will be greater than those of the one who remains in the family home with the children. Because you won't have the familiar family demands and responsibilities and you are starting a new life, keeping the attachment between yourself and the children will require more effort. But do:

- Get your new quarters in order as soon as possible, if only to reassure the children that their relationship with you continues, that you are still their parent, and that you live the kind of organized life they are used to.
- Use the phone to let the children know you are settled and say good night.
- Remember that cooking skills are not gender-related —for you or your kids. Learn and/or teach them. Or do both together.
- Let the kids help you select any furnishings and equipment you need to buy, at least for the room or rooms they will occupy when they visit you.
- Help kids establish friendships with children in your building or neighborhood. Throwing a ball around outside or walking around the neighborhood or exploring nearby parks are good ways to meet other kids.

Realize you will have feelings of loss. After all, you are leaving behind the daily relationship not only with your ex-spouse, but with your children as well. Many parents don't miss leaving their spouse nearly as much as they miss leaving their children.

*Leaving was hard—and still is, every time I take the boys
back to the house after our time together on the weekend.
Seeing the dog there, too—my dog. And the house we had
built that I was so proud of. The day she asked me for my
keys to our house stands out in my mind. I just have to
detach myself or it hurts too much. I guess I look insensi-
tive but if I don't, the leaving becomes too difficult.*

—Walt Tornow, Plymouth, MN

The House Key

Probably nothing is as significant as the now out-of-
the-house parent's handing over the key to the house
or apartment. It's as hard for one spouse to ask for
the key as it is for the other to hand it over or at
least let you know it will not be used again. Many
women are afraid to ask for the key, feeling "it's his
house, too." But it's important to address the "key"
issue as soon as possible after you separate. Leaving
the house with one's belongings is a statement that
one adult has left the home. Returning unannounced
or while the home is empty is no longer appropriate. Holding on to the key is holding onto what now
must become one's past. Handing over—or asking
for—the key is an important step toward the acceptance of the present. It's important to ask for the key
if it has not been forthcoming. Ask, don't demand.
If refused, just have your locks changed. This sounds
like a small act but it's a large emotional hurdle.
Keep in mind, though, that it will have to be done
eventually and that it really is one of the more
clear-cut moves to implement in this divorcing
process.

THE FIRST WEEK

Although some families find it comparatively easy to cope with the parent's departure, others find that the reality that sinks in that first week can be surprisingly hard to handle. Preparation doesn't stop children (and adults) from feeling stunned. There is often an overwhelming feeling of deep sadness—unlike any other you've experienced. Meals and evenings seem lonely and depressing. People phone, wanting to know what happened, or to give support. It's generally a long, sad, and confusing week. Sometimes you don't hear people who speak to you. You feel "spacey," or tears suddenly appear in your eyes. You stare at book pages without reading words. The "whys" keep floating around in your mind. And the big question: *When will this pain go away?* (It will, it will. Believe me.)

If you have become unglued, give yourself some credit. You are dealing with the pain now. You won't have to do it again later. Many adults repress their pain only to find that it surfaces down the road. Sooner or later, the anger and sadness must be released.

Things Kids Need that First Week

These things *do* make a difference to children:

- Getting enough information about what is happening and why.
- Encouraging contact with the parent who has left.
- Knowing where you'll be, how they can reach you, and that they are free to use the phone frequently to reach the other parent, if they wish.
- Knowing they can talk about the absent parent (even though you may wish they wouldn't!).
- Seeing parents behaving with courtesy and respect to each other.

- Being spared most of your anger and emotional swings. Going out for a car ride alone, or locking yourself in the bathroom where you can cry, or making private phone calls are ways you can do this.
- Allowing their strong feelings of hurt to surface—with your understanding that it is an important and healthy part of the grieving process.
- Hearing parents talking about their feelings and sharing some aspects of their grief with their children. Reassuring the children that you can take care of yourself and will take good care of them even if you're sad, angry, or upset.
- Being told again it's not their fault.
- Being told they are loved, they're terrific, and you're glad they are yours.

How can a child like himself or herself when the parent doesn't or doesn't verbalize these feelings? How can a child feel loved—not abandoned—if he's ignored or out of touch with either parent at this difficult time? Always being away from one parent is the most difficult adjustment for children. They are unsure how they will be "shared," and how often they'll see each parent is an unknown. But, once the new arrangements become a routine that can be trusted, children do adjust.

The breakfast table now seemed strained and lonely with just the three of us there. The following week while we were shopping, we wandered into a pet store. Suddenly we were the proud owners of two parakeets and a cage. It turned our eating area into a lively place and gave it a new focus. It marked the beginning of our new history as a family.

—Unsigned

Because this is not an easy time, promise yourself
that you will not make any important decisions that
you don't have to make for at least six months, if not a
year. Don't move, don't remodel the kitchen, don't
remarry, don't change jobs. Don't be in a rush. The
future will reveal itself with time. Significant decisions bring more changes and more stress. For now,
one day at a time is a lot . . . and all you need to deal
with.

THE FANTASY OF RECONCILIATION

Most children harbor the wish that their divorced
parents will get back together again, until, of course,
ties are completely severed when one remarries—and
even then it can persist. (After all, if the parents divorced once, it can happen again.) Young children are
likely to make wild promises that they'll be everlast-
ingly good if only you'll live together again, and their
wishes on birthday cake candles and "first star I see
tonight" are likely to center on the reunited family.
Older ones may learn the futility of talking about it,
but they often fantasize about the ideal family and
selectively recall the events of their former "happy
perfect" family life.

Helping to Lay the Fantasy to Rest

This may not be easy to do, but the following will
help:

• Not telling your children one parent will be leaving
  long before the event is to take place. The kids need
  a little notice, but not so much that they think you
  may have changed your minds.

- Asking the children periodically if they still think you and your former spouse will reunite. This is a good time to discuss your relationship with your spouse, explain to a younger child it's possible to love someone you don't live with, and that relationships and people change.
- Treating your former spouse with civility, but not with familiarity when the children are present, so there will be no doubt in their minds about the relationship between you.
- Helping children understand some specific reasons why you are divorcing, if you and your spouse didn't have visible conflict before or after the separation. Children of a "good" divorce sometimes think that because you "get along," you might get back together.
- Not spending the night with your former spouse—or not letting the children know if you have.

Most children will have an ongoing, intense longing for a reunited family, even when they do not expect this to occur. A 1983 study showed that custody arrangements did not affect this longing. Children want and wish for an intact family for a long time. Your acceptance of their feelings of longing (versus a denial or put-down of them) can do a lot to help your children come to grips with their loss of this fantasy. Use language like, "I know you wish that Mommy (Daddy) and I would get back together again, but it's not going to happen. Wishing for it is something you can't help feeling, and it's okay. I understand." Your child's fantasy of reunion (as long as it is not an obsessive delusion) is not a sign of a maladjusted child. Even for adults, there are times when a bit of fantasy is helpful.

If Reconciliation Is a Possibility

Yes, many parents do reconcile after separation. Always let kids know what is going on. Keep them updated on any and all outings, even if they are only cordial and uneventful. But keep in mind that it's important not to yo-yo your children's feelings with back-and-forth possibilities. Children may "invent" a reuniting scene unless they have information to the contrary. If the return of the other parent rests on preset conditions (such as no more alcohol use), don't keep these conditions secret from the children. They will then know that if the reconciliation doesn't work, they're not to blame. And remember:

- Don't ask children if they "want" Daddy (Mommy) back. It's not their decision. They need to know that whatever they want or say won't affect the success or failure of a reconciliation—it's a matter for adults.
- Be sure your trial relationship is extensive enough before returning to your prior family ways. It may help not only to "date" your spouse but even to take a vacation together prior to reuniting.
- If Daddy or Mommy is "sleeping over," explain to the kids that this doesn't promise a reconciliation.
- Let children know that you are working on the relationship but you don't know if it's permanent. Take your time to find out.
- For a trial reconciliation, your best response is an honest one. "We're trying this. We'll all have to see how it goes," is a reasonable announcement, if it accurately reflects your situation.

As a general rule of thumb, except for your sexual conduct,

IF IT'S GOOD FOR YOU, IT'S
GOOD FOR YOUR KIDS.

If One Parent Wants to Reconcile and the Other Doesn't

Potentially this is a very dangerous situation because it will be natural—and devastating—for one parent to use the children to reach the other spouse. The noncustodial parent may hope to be taken back when the other parent sees "how much the children want him or her back." Statements like this keep children's reunion fantasy alive when it's not realistic, and therefore, it is unfair.

It's not uncommon for this situation to occur when one spouse initiates the separation; the other—after regrouping from the initial shock—begins to change and move ahead with his or her life, then becomes interesting once again to the person who asked for the divorce. Any reconciliation at this point has to be between adults only. Making children messengers and responsible for getting the family together is a terrible burden. And the children suffer for it.

What you *can* do in this situation is:

- Enlist your spouse's understanding of the situation. Perhaps that parent can be encouraged to attend a family counseling session to get a third party point of view.
- Seek out family counseling to allow everyone to sort feelings and expectations.
- Let your children hear you acknowledge and validate their feelings with words such as, "Josh, this must be very hard for you," or "I'd feel angry/mad, if I were you, too."
- Explain to your children that nobody is to blame, especially not them, if Mom and Dad can't rekindle their romance and desire to live together. There is nothing they can do about it. Nothing! Whatever

caused the initial separation was just a symptom of a long-standing unhappiness that each parent is just now coming to grips with.

Be sure they know that they don't have to choose between parents and that both parents will always love them. And remember

YOU CAN'T PUSH ANYONE
TOWARD YOU.

4

Words Matter: Learning "Divorce-Speak"

Knowing how to yell, demand, and vent anger may come naturally. However, shifting gears into a new divorce-speak management style takes some learning.

HOW TO TALK ABOUT THE DEPARTING SPOUSE TO YOUR CHILDREN

Anger and frustration toward your spouse are normal emotions and you'll need to vent them—*but not in front of the children!* It *is* possible to detest your spouse and still not fight when it comes to your children. *It's done every day.*

It's an understatement to say that it's difficult to take at face value your spouse's statements of good intentions when you'd far rather tell the kids how irresponsible and unfair he or she is. If the exiting spouse does hurtful things and doesn't live up to his or her responsibilities, there is no need to point this out to the children. They will come to their own conclusions as they grow up. In the long run, it will be impossible to fool the children. But in the beginning children *need* to believe in and love both parents. Don't deny them that.

What's vital, but not easy to say is: "Your dad (mom) will always be your dad (mom); you will now have two homes."

87

Language to Keep in Mind

- "Your dad (mom) and I feel differently about . . ."
- "It sounds like you need to talk to your dad (mom) about that."
- "I don't know if it's wrong or right but I feel . . . , think . . . ,"
- "You can disagree with your dad (mom) but still love him/her."
- "You might not get what you want but it is your right and responsibility to ask for it."
- "I have a hard time dealing with your father (mother). Bear with me."
- "I'm feeling sad (or lonely, alone, etc.) at the moment. Just give me a little time to myself. Thank you. I love you."
- "No, I don't love mom (dad) now, but I did when we married and had you, and that's what's important."
- "I can't answer that. You'll have to ask your dad (mom)."
- "I'm not sure how to answer that. Let me think about it and we'll discuss it later. Remind me if I forget; I want to answer but I'm sad right now."
- "I don't know why your dad (mom) feels/acts that way."
- "You can't make someone love you or anyone else."
- "I know how much you miss your father (mother)."
- "Perhaps he (she) can't help him (herself) right now but it's nothing you did."
- "Your dad (mom) has many wonderful qualities. That's why I married him/her in the first place."
- "Your dad (mom) did not leave us. He (she) left our marriage. He (she) didn't want to stop being with you so we will work on ways that you two will keep on seeing each other."
- "Don't ever believe that because your father (mother) fell out of love with me, that he (she) doesn't love you anymore."

Remember that when you attack a child's parent, it will feel to that child like you are attacking the child. It might not seem logical to you but it's the only way a child is able to feel.

It was most difficult—but most important—to let them and their father develop a healthy relationship with no sabotaging from me. If I demeaned him, then I was demeaning a part of them. This was especially true because my children were boys and their father was their main role model. I managed to find the inner strength to keep my frustrations to myself, to listen without undue comment to theirs, to share in their good visitation times, and even to come to their father's defense where they were concerned. Kids are masters at setting us up as bait. I'd have none of that.
—Barbara Mindel, Poughkeepsie, NY

KEEPING YOUR COOL

Watch what you say. Keep an eye on your body language. Your threats, sarcasms, and put-downs are harmful to a child already living with insecurity and fear of abandonment. These will, in the long run, damage your relationship with your child. After all, no matter how low, despicable, unthinking, lazy, abusive, or cheap your ex was or is, a child will still want to love that parent. As a child matures, he or she can decide whether that love or adoration should continue without any input from you. From our own adult perspective, we can recognize that often it is long into adulthood until we are able to think less of a parent without thinking less of ourselves.

Our popular culture has enshrined the belief that leveling or "telling it like it is" and expressing anger is the only honest form of communication. We have come a long way in learning the truth about that old saying,

"Sticks and stones may break my bones but words can never hurt me"—they can and they do. Take responsibility for the consequences of your verbalized honesty and anger.

Stop Yourself When You Find Yourself Saying

- *If you don't behave, I'll send you to live with your father (or mother).*
- *You're lazy (stubborn or bad tempered) just like your mother (or father).*
- *I could get along better here by myself.*
- *If you weren't here, I could . . .*
- *Someday you'll leave me too, just like your mother (father), or its variation, Promise me you'll never leave.*
- *Your mother (father) put you up to saying that.*
- *Your dad (mom) doesn't love any of us or he (she) wouldn't have left us.*
- *You can't trust him (her)!*
- *That bastard (bitch)!*
- *If he (she) loved you, he (she) would pay your support checks, right? (variation: end sentence with "on time.")*
- *Sometimes I wish I'd been the one to skip out.*
- *If you don't like what I buy you, ask your father (mother) to do better.*
- *Who would you really rather be with, Mommy or Daddy?*
- *What is your father (mother) saying about me?*
- *Now that you're the "man of the house" ("the little mother") . . .*
- *You're all I have. You are the only person I can rely on.*
- *He (she) was just no good.*
- *If it wasn't for you, your father (mother) would still be here.*
- *If your father (mother) is five minutes late again, you're just not going with him (her).*
- *Over my dead body!*

Some things your children do may remind you of your former spouse, and these actions may unconsciously (or consciously) make you feel angry. This is a normal reaction, but catch yourself before you act on these feelings. It's unfair to unload on your kids. Your child is *not* your ex. Not only will you strain your relationship with your child by "unloading," but you will diminish your child's self-esteem. By the same token, beware of using your kids to get even with your spouse. You may well be teaching them a lesson that will backfire as they learn how to play one parent off against the other. Don't act as though your child's other parent doesn't exist. Your spouse may no longer belong to you, but he or she will always be your child's father or mother.

When in doubt about how to respond to any situation, put yourself in your child's place. Imagine how you would feel if your parents said or did what you are about to say or do. Let *that* guide your behavior.

HOW TO TALK *TO* YOUR EXITING SPOUSE

When in doubt as to how to act toward your spouse, think about how you would respond to a total stranger in a given situation and then act accordingly. You would not hang up the phone at the sound of a stranger or glare at a new person for saying hello or asking about your health. When you must confer with your ex-spouse:

- Stop talking for a while if you find that an argument is beginning.
- Try not to start sentences with the word *you*. Rather begin with words like "I feel . . ."

- Use goal-setting as a way of talking about the children. Summer plans or academic programs are usually a good focus for discussion.
- When it's important to get together, meet on neutral ground. A quiet restaurant will probably force you to temper your volume.

Give Him or Her the Benefit of the Doubt

Don't assume a "NO." Parents often fail to ask the other parent about many things on the assumption that the answer will be "no!" The worst that can happen is that that other parent will say no, which is your assumption anyway, so why not ask? And there may be things you can ask now that you would not have felt comfortable about asking six months ago, such as a one-time school activity pickup when the children are at your house. Don't let your own assumptions handicap you. Many a parent has been known to shift a schedule, pick up a child, attend a school event, or even pay for something that hadn't been anticipated—because they were asked! Remember, it's important that the question be asked adult to adult, not angry spouse to angry spouse. Your tone and your manner count. And everyone benefits. If you are assuming (or getting) a "NO" in the heat of separation, be willing to try again six months from now.

When You Can't Talk to Your Spouse

Many couples find themselves unable to communicate in person or on the phone with their exiting spouses. This is a tremendous loss on many different levels. It complicates issues; it has a spillover effect on the children (how would you have felt if your parents couldn't handle a simple phone call to meet your needs?); it puts a strain on parenting effectiveness; and it offers children the chance to play you off against each other. Being a parent is a business. As in any business, you don't have to like all the aspects about it. You no longer have to live with your ex, but must deal with him or her on occasion. At first you will be interacting frequently, but after some time, it will taper off. If tempers are still volatile but contact is important—to set schedules, for example—use the mail. It's a less emotional way to communicate.

But months later, if you can't talk to your spouse— meaning that you can't call—*you have a problem.* You are angry and hiding behind it. If you can't deal with your anger, do search out a counselor to help you see how you are hurting yourself. (An ex-spouse is seldom hurt by not hearing from you.) On the other hand, if your ex hangs up on you when you call, send this book to him or her and hope for the best.

WHEN A CHILD WON'T VISIT OR TALK TO THE OTHER PARENT

Some children will announce that they "hate" the other parent and refuse to visit Mom or Dad. Deep down, the child is confused about whether love or hate is the proper emotion. One can't really "hate" someone he or she doesn't love or care about intensely. Hate keeps another alive for you. Apathy, polite concern, and lack of strong emotions toward another is true detachment. (Keep this thought in mind for yourself if you're dealing poorly with an exiting spouse.)

If you are a parent rejected by your child, try to understand that some children cope by defining or labeling one parent as "bad" because it gives them a place to dump their anger. With time and your constant approaches—regardless of the negative behavior you may have to endure—perceptions will change.

Children need to love each parent, even the one they choose to regard as the "bad one."

Sometimes a child doesn't want to see the absent parent only because it conflicts with another activity. Activities and visiting with friends should not take precedence over a relationship with a parent that needs to be worked at, and certainly not without the other parent's consent. As children reach adolescence this will change. Sometimes a child does have a personality conflict with the other parent, and visits may be downright unpleasant. Or visits may just be boring. There may be a very impersonal reason, such as the feeling of an illness coming on. And yes, occasionally it *is* because a child is discouraged from visiting by the other parent.

If your child doesn't want to spend time with the other parent, it is important to let him or her know this is not an option, even if this makes you feel somewhat vindicated in not liking your spouse. This is especially important with a young child. Ask your child to verbalize his or her reasons. Listen carefully. Do you detect anger, a loyalty bind, an unrealistic interpretation of adult words? It is possible that some joint family counseling should be explored in order to clear the air and get a third party's perspective on the situation. Sometimes when there is more than one child, time alone with the other parent is a remedy. Perhaps the ex-spouse visiting in the custodial home could solve the problem.

There will be times and situations when you will have to back your child's not wanting to see the other parent, but these should be related to abusive conditions —emotional or physical, or serious personality differences or problems. Sometimes a child's rejection of a parent can be a healthy response to an unhealthy relationship. At the same time, be wary of classifying the other parent as a "bad influence" as a reason to discourage time together. An occasional instance of poor judgment on the part of one parent should be kept in perspective. With time and maturity even the most trying of relationships tend to swing back into perspective and some sort of harmony.

As children reach their teens, their personal relationships with each parent will come into play. Each teen has times of not talking to a parent even when a family is living together; this also occurs within restructured families. Knowing when hostilities are hormonal in nature is one of the finer lines to decipher.

WHEN THE OTHER PARENT WON'T COMMUNICATE WITH HIS OR HER CHILDREN

This is a tough one. It's hard to be generous when you've been abandoned. Be honest. Share your feelings of hurt and anger with your children, but explain that the other parent is a different person now from the one you married. Help your children not to take this neglect as a personal rejection—and they will need a lot of help here. If at all possible:

- Acknowledge feelings of hurt and loss.
- Remind them it is not their fault that this has happened. Sometimes adults have personality problems that limit their ability to love and show responsibility —but that doesn't mean that a child is any less lovable.
- Don't build false hopes that the parent will change and will soon be in touch regularly.
- Point out all those people who love and care for your child. *All* these people can't be wrong!
- Accept expressions of your child's feelings of rage and hurt. It prevents that scarring that comes with repressed anger.

Time doesn't make a child's lack of contact with an absent parent easier. Be sensitive to ongoing hurt feelings.

Sometimes mothers or fathers who lose custody feel they've lost face, and therefore remove themselves physically and emotionally from the whole situation because partial contact is just too painful. Unfortunately, children don't understand or care to understand this. They only know that they have been left and they feel rejected. Also, when a noncustodial parent distances him or herself after a painful family split, it is often to lick "psychological wounds" before reentering and taking on an active parenting role. For some, this will take a few months; for others it may be a few years.

What if the absent parent returns years later? Keep your anger out of the way. Children look for any chance to mend their bridges with a parent. And who knows what changes have occurred? Children are entitled to look and see for themselves.

Grief Makes Some People Tender and Compassionate, and Others—Not As Strong Perhaps—It Makes Hard, Encased in Protective Armor.
—Maxwell Maltz

THE OPTION OF "THE OTHER HOUSE"

One of the best and worst parts of having parents with separate homes is that the fantasy of safely running away from, or being banished to the other "home" (a safe and acceptable alternative), becomes a reality. A child can "leave" one parent to live with the other parent without leaving "home." And for the parent wishing for the child to "be gone," there is now a realistic alternative to putting the child out on the street.

The threat "If you don't like it here, leave!" surfaces, if not on parents' lips, then certainly in their hearts on occasion. It is usually felt in response to your children's words, "I hate you. I'm going to live with Dad (Mom)." Hard as this threat is to hear from your child, do not respond to it emotionally. Tempting though it may be to say "So go then," restrain yourself. Children need to learn the difference between flight and fight. Let them know that it is not an acceptable alternative to leave when the going gets rough. Plus, all children need to feel secure and wanted. It's not easy for children to be Ping-Pong balls in an emotionally charged table tennis game, even if they have set themselves up for it.

We made the rule that one house was not a place to go when the kid was "in trouble" in the other house. Unfinished business (curfews, grounding, undone jobs) had to be cleared up first.
> *—Lee Mauk, Minneapolis, MN*

A NEW KIND OF PARENTING PARTNERSHIP

UNLIKE MARRIAGE, MOST DIVORCES LAST FOREVER.

For the sake of your kids, make sure your divorce works well. Your relationship with your former spouse will need redefining. Ideally, you'll learn to give the other parent the benefit of the doubt and to trust him or her in certain situations because you have the same goal—to provide the best lives you can for your kids. This person may now be acting like a monster . . . an ogre . . . a dragon, but you married him or her and at one time you saw the good qualities. These qualities may no longer be demonstrated to you but are probably available to your children.

Violating your divorce decree can become a cold war tactic. War—hot or cold—is *not* what you need if you wish to get on with your life. Therefore, it's best to:

• Work at developing a new kind of language—nonjudgmental, factual, and neutral—to use with your ex-spouse when you discuss the kids. Be civil and as friendly as you can, and be careful to avoid sexual overtones and former intimacies of wording or manner.

• Bring up what you perceive to be problems, try to reach common ground, and show a willingness to compromise. Stick to the topic in discussions; don't bring up old grievances or matters that have nothing to do with the kids.

• Discuss money issues and parenting issues in separate phone calls.

• Dishing out blame when problems arise is an easy but cheap shot. Concentrate on solutions and compromise.

• Don't jump at the opportunity to make your ex look bad—and you will probably have many!

• Figure out before you begin to talk just what it is you want of the other parent and express your wishes fully and clearly. Try writing out your "speech" beforehand if you're afraid you'll forget important points or get sidetracked.

• Pick your time carefully for discussing topics you know to be inflammatory. Listen carefully to the other parent's answers or statements and watch for nonverbal clues such as clenched fists or pursed lips. Back off if you can see you're getting nowhere, and try again another time.

- Remember that your spouse's "character flaws" will not disappear when you divorce. The things that bothered you before will still bother you now. Luckily, you will be dealing with them less—but they will continue to surface over the years.
- Approach your new relationship with the other parent as a business partnership. You are partners in a business. The assets are your children.

TRY TO PRESENT A UNITED FRONT TO THE KIDS ON IMPORTANT ISSUES. KEEP THEM OUT OF THE MIDDLE.

I remember how hard it was for my mom when my parents divorced. A single parent should include the kids in as much as possible—it helps them feel part of a family and not that they are a burden and unwanted by the parent.

—Bessie Dobbs, Lakeville, MN

A certificate of divorce does not prohibit you from contacting the other parent to discuss your child's needs. Do it when necessary and do it *well*—for the sake of your children and your peace of mind.

Strangely enough, being civil and cooperative, important as it is, also has a hidden negative. The children may not understand why you have divorced if you can get along and why you won't reconcile now. It's important to share the reasons for your divorce off and on, down the road, when your children mistake courtesy (or even friendship) for viability in a marriage. Again, when there is no apparent reason for a divorce—no open hostility—remember who may assume they're responsible. That's right, your children. At the very least, they may be angry with you for divorcing "when you really can get along."

5

The Issues: Money, Legalities, Custody

In a divorce, there is usually one area that becomes a focal point or battleground. It may be money, the family pet, a household possession, or custody. Try to see your power struggles clearly. Many custody cases are really about money—not custody. Divorce is a lose-lose situation for adults and children. If you really need to do battle over something, be sure it is not the children.

These issues are hardest for the person who is left in the marriage. The person who initiates the uncoupling usually has a life plan; the one being left seldom does.

MONEY MATTERS

Money can become one of the most important and disruptive issues in a divorce. The central money issue for women is the fear that they won't be able to survive financially even when there is money available, and the issue is exacerbated when money is in short supply. Overall, the time of divorce and separation is scary. For the majority of American families, the decision of the parents to separate and divorce will mean that children will experience a significant decline in their standard of living; the exceptions are

101

the children of the very wealthy or the very poor. The average family's standard of living cannot be maintained when there are two households. The same income, for the most part, will now be needed to finance two separate households.

It would be nice to be able to say that custody concerns and money concerns are separate issues. This is true legally, but the reality is different. One study found 56 percent of mothers with sole custody returned to court because their ex-husbands refused to pay child support. (Interestingly, there were no mothers with joint custody in this study who had returned to court for child support matters.) Don't confuse custody—sole or joint—with child support. Child support is a financial arrangement. Custody has to do with caring for a child. Ultimately the arrangements are based on what the parents can agree upon, what the lawyers will settle for, or what a judge decides. The unfortunate reality is that no two individuals ever seem able to agree on what is fair or reasonable when it comes to dividing resources.

EQUITABLE IS NOT ALWAYS EQUAL.

Money has emotional overtones as well as undeniably real ramifications. Children may view a lack of financial support and a reduction in life-style as a parent's loss of love and trust. It's hard for a mother or father to feel good about her or his children's relationship with the other parent if that person left them floundering financially. And parents trying to cope with the loss of respect from their children when funds are tight (or when they are being tight with funds), struggle, too.

If there is bitterness from the start, money disagreements will usually follow the lines of anger. Again, it is the children who suffer. If he is not satisfied with visitation arrangements, a man may use money as a weapon by making support payments late or withholding them altogether. Mothers, on the other hand, have been known to make access to the children difficult when payments are not made on time. Both of these methods are illegal and unfair to children.

If money was an issue in your marriage, it will most likely be a *BIG* issue in your divorce. Money is a symbol that often goes beyond the actual dollars and cents involved. If you were married and the major income earner lost his or her job, you would make the necessary adjustments. Unfortunately, you must keep this in mind in a divorce, too. As long as you will be receiving child-support payments, you will be sharing the down—as well as the up—side of your former spouse's income. Thus, you cannot look to child support as a concrete form of security or income. Conversely, if your children are young, it is important to build in a cost-of-living provision, because it is only fair that each parent share in the cost of inflation, as well as the rising expenses associated with teenagers.

Separation is a time when you will start separating financially. This will mean setting up new checking or saving accounts, making changes on credit cards, making financial decisions without having someone to share in those decisions. You need to become familiar with your tax returns (yes, you *can* understand them—if not the first time, then you will by the second or third time round)—as well as medical insurance benefits and payments. For the uninitiated, this is usually new and often difficult, but it does get easier with practice. Separation is also a time of growing mistrust between separating spouses as you begin to have different vested interests. That is a normal, albeit unfortunate, spillover of separation and divorce. Keep in mind that knowledge of all financial matters—yours and your exiting spouse's—is important and should not be ignored in the pain of your separation. A family's separation usually occurs quickly. Money issues can last for years. It is important to keep these matters between the adults involved, so that children are not subject to the ongoing insecurity of their parent's financial battles.

Money issues seem to bring out the worst in people. More times than not, the saying that "If you don't hate him (her) now, you will before this is over," is all too accurate.

Today, maintenance or spousal support (alimony) for a wife, even a traditional homemaker, is more difficult to get for more than a few years if you are young. A marriage license does not translate into a perpetual pension, especially if you are young enough and able enough to work or learn new job skills. Thus, for many women, negotiations for good child-support terms have become more important. Still, it's important to understand that the current thrust of laws for the raising of children and paying child-related expenses is in the direction of a joint responsibility.

WHAT DOES CHILD SUPPORT COVER?

What child support covers is often hard to separate from support of the custodial parent. Paying for a roof over your child's head means paying for the roof over the former spouse's head, too. Men often feel their former wives are spending support payments frivolously and battles intensify. The issue is not simple, and it seldom seems fair to either side.

I cannot emphasize enough how important it is to get a carefully worded and detailed court order in the area of child support. Don't let your lawyer agree to a dollar amount alone. Terms should be spelled out. For instance, does the child-support payment cover the children's medical and dental insurance as well, or will that be separate? Will there be a cost-of-living increase clause? Support groups such as ACES (see page 115) will help educate you in this area.

Even in joint custody arrangements wherein parents have drawn up careful schedules for sharing normal expenses, new expenses arise continuously. How does one deal with those one-time, large, nonbudgeted expenses, like braces, glasses, special tutoring, sports equipment, and the real biggie—college tuition? And the older your kids get, the more it costs to support them. Raising children is expensive and the noncustodial parent must be aware that all those one-time expenses add up.

Generally, parents are not legally responsible for paying college costs. Still, a court may order a noncustodial parent to pay college costs if a combination of factors indicates that financial ability and previous expectation for such has been shown.

IT'S AGAINST THE LAW NOT TO SUPPORT ONE'S CHILDREN.

What is typical for child-support payments? Unfortunately, there is no uniform answer. Every family is unique. Incomes, prior living styles, physical, emotional, and educational needs, parents' resources—all must be taken into account. Your lawyer or mediator will be able to give you an idea of what's common in your state (most have certain guidelines) given your net worth and income(s). The Census Bureau reported the average national child-support payment in 1985 to be $2,215 annually. One rule of thumb is 25 percent of the noncustodial's take-home pay at the time of your divorce will go to child support. But only a professional can tell you whether this will be applicable for you. Don't rely on stories by friends and neighbors.

Second marriages often suffer because of the pressure of payments to the first family. The second wife is usually well aware of her husband's obligation, but resentments can grow with time, nonetheless. In theory, a second wife's income is not taken into account regarding financial arrangements for a man's first family, but often it is because it affects his lifestyle. If a child is born into the second marriage, everyone concerned may suffer financially. In the cases of multiple marriages, the issue of money becomes even more confusing as parents negotiate their financial responsibility to children, stepchildren, and former stepchildren. Another important question to be addressed is this: Given all these variations and combinations, who should be listed in one's will?

"She expected nothing from him but trouble. Already that was a help. Once she ceased expecting, she ceased being angry . . . for anger is really disappointed hope."
—Erica Jong in Parachutes and Kisses (NAL)

Middle-class women whose husbands' salaries are high and whose own work experience is limited suffer the greatest drop in income after divorce in what is sometimes referred to as "the feminization of poverty." Lenore Weitzman, in her book *The Divorce Revolution* (The Free Press, 1986), claims that the average divorced woman suffers a 73 percent decline in her standard of living in the first year, whereas that of her former husband increases by 42 percent. Before you panic, you should know that several experts have disputed this number, claiming it is based on obsolete data and inaccurate methodology. Still, the basic premise of greatly reduced income for divorcing women stands.

The House Divided

It's a common practice for the home to go to the wife in divorce. Sometimes women fail to get good advice on the tax aspects of receiving the family home. Women over the age of 55 may lose half of the one-time $125,000 capital gain exclusion. Also, a couple who agrees to split the proceeds from the sale of a house (often after the children are no longer living there) will be tied together until long after their divorce. Don't rush into any significant decisions, such as how to deal with the family home, without receiving good advice and adequate time to weigh all the implications.

THE PAYING PARENT

Writing a check each month to one's former spouse for child support is usually a painful act. Child support often feels like alimony maintenance when it comes to writing that check. But child support is more than money—something the noncustodial parent seldom understands. It carries with it an emotional commitment to one's children and is perceived in this light by the custodial parent and child. That is why late or unreceived child-support payments lead to heightened financial difficulties because of the anger and fear of abandonment that is felt.

Child-support payments are over and above the amount of money needed when the children are spending time with the noncustodial parent. Child-support payments assume that the paying parent will have his or her own child-related expenses; you can't deduct out-of-pocket costs from child support. Custodial parents have fixed costs for the kids, no matter where the kids are on a given day. If the children spend extended time with the noncustodial parent, support agreements can change. This cannot be done as a unilateral move, however.

Any number of fractured families spend April playing the game called, "Who Gets the Kids as a Tax Deduction?"
—Ellen Goodman, The Boston Globe, April 15, 1988

If You Are the Less Well-Off Parent

In marriage, spouses share a life-style. If there's money for luxuries, both enjoy them. In divorce, after the assets are divided, one parent—most often the husband, and the one with whom the child spends the least time—usually ends up with more discretionary income than the other. If you're the one who has little or no money for luxuries, it's normal for you to be angry about this apparent unfairness. It's unhealthy and ultimately damaging for you to *stay* angry about it, however.

Financial inequity exists because society, at any given time, values certain activities more than others. This does not mean that one parent works less hard than the other or is a less productive person. The parent with less income will have to overcome feelings of competitiveness and inadequacy. Children are also more likely to prefer to spend their time where there are more "things." This is a normal reaction and doesn't mean you are loved or valued less. And children may resent the life-style of the wealthier parent if they have to live with fewer luxuries. You may be jealous when your better-off ex does things with and buys gifts for your child that you cannot afford to do and buy. "Saturday Santas" try to compensate for limited time spent with their kids. Absence from everyday routine often works to the advantage of the noncustodial parent, and you may feel hurt when he (or she) appears to be put on a pedestal by your child.

Custodial parents prefer the visiting parent to give time and affection rather than gifts and perceived extravagance to children. But noncustodial parents feel the need to do special things to make up for their limited time with their kids. It's important to put a leash on your judgmental views, and to be appreciative of the fact that he or she does all these seemingly inappropriate things. Think of the alternative!

Force yourself, if necessary, to express interest in that glorious time your child has had with the other parent. If you allow your irritation or jealousy to show, the child will become defensive and protective of the other parent and feel guilty about loving him or her. In other words, your child will once again be caught in the middle of *your* problem.

If You Are the Better-Off Parent

Try to understand that your ex-spouse may resent your comparative wealth. If there are things you can do to help financially, try to do so. You don't want to be taken advantage of, but added help with extra expenses can go a long way to lessen the difficulties of your children. Many children are concerned about college expenses and many a dad who would gladly pay for college for the kids if he were still married to their mom will not do so after the divorce. Remember: <u>You divorced your spouse, not your children.</u> Some parents divide the expenses of the children based on the income of the parents. Thus, the parent who earns twice as much pays twice as many of the expenses. Parents who have joint custody are more likely to make these kinds of arrangements.

Know Your Terms and
Their Tax Consequences

MAINTENANCE or SPOUSAL SUPPORT (Alimony):
payment of support by one spouse to another in
satisfaction of marital obligations
- is taxable, periodic income (versus a lump sum)
  to the recipient and a tax deduction for the one
  who pays it—providing:
    (a) it is paid in cash under the terms of a writ-
        ten agreement or a divorce decree, and
    (b) that the couple does not live in the same
        house or file a joint return;
- is considered earned income for the purpose of
  qualifying for an IRA;
- ends upon the death of the paying spouse
  (The tax law is quite precise about what alimony
  is and isn't so that it can't be "hidden" in child
  support or a property settlement.)

CHILD SUPPORT: monthly sums paid by a divorced
parent for the continued medical, educational, and
financial needs of the child
- is not taxable to the receiving parent nor deductible for the paying parent. (If a former spouse
  moves to another state, an order filed in one state
  can be carried out in another state.)

CLAIMING CHILDREN AS EXEMPTIONS: the $2000
(as of 1989) per child exemption can be claimed by
the parent having custody for the greater part of the
year. This exemption can be claimed by the noncustodial parent when
- The custodial parent signs an authorizing waiver
  that the noncustodial parent attaches to his or
  her tax return;
- or if your agreement was signed prior to 1985,
  the noncustodial parent contributes $600 annu-
  ally to a child's support.

(Giving the exemption credit to the noncustodial parent does not affect the custodial parent's right to claim head-of-household status.)

MEDICAL EXPENSES
- can be deducted by the noncustodial parent who pays them and be taxable to the custodial parent not paying for them.

PROPERTY SETTLEMENTS
- are transferred with no taxable gain or loss for the recipient;
- are usually lump-sum payments or property transfers.

(When the asset transferred is property, it is always in the best interest of the person transferring property to give a low-basis property that has appreciated—the high tax liability is therefore passed along. Conversely, it is always in the best interest of the recipient to take a high-basis property so as not to get hit with a high tax bill when the property is sold.)

LEGAL FEES
- are not tax deductible in connection with a divorce or determining child support or child custody;
- are usually paid separately by each of those involved;
- are deductible if you are seeking or receiving alimony (be sure your lawyer itemizes the bill, separating all alimony-related costs).

STATUTORY REQUIREMENTS
- can set aside even a mutually agreeable stipulation in whole or in part if it doesn't meet your state's requirements. This is especially true in interstate cases.

*While vacationing in the Caribbean, a friend met a very
nice couple. The man had been married before. His new
wife said that whenever they took a vacation, they gave
the same kind of vacation to his ex-wife. When my friend
expressed her amazement at their generosity, they said it
was a good investment. She could not afford those kinds
of vacations on her own, and they did not want her
resentment over their better circumstances to sour her
relationship with them.*

—Unsigned

THE REALITY OF NONSUPPORT

Many noncustodial parents avoid paying their fair
share of the costs involved in raising their children.
Statistics differ, but a 1985 Census Bureau survey indicated that fewer than half the women eligible for
child-support payments were getting them. In 1985
only two million of the nine million women raising
their children alone received full child-support payments. Recent state and federal legislation is helping,
but more effective laws are required. One new law
allows the Internal Revenue Service to deduct overdue
support payments from returns due to taxpayers. Current local and county family support units accept cases,
not only for the poor, but for families in which a
nonpaying parent has moved out of state. In low-income
families, fathers often officially leave their homes to
enable spouses to qualify for welfare payments. Encouraging fatherhood must be approached in new ways
to enable shared financial responsibility.

Only 10 percent of the men eligible for support
receive it. Contrary to cultural stereotypes, many sole
custodial fathers also need child support.

Sad But True

- On the average, a woman's income decreases 73 percent after a divorce.
- Eighty-five percent of divorced women receive no alimony or spousal support.
- Twenty-six percent of divorced mothers never receive any child support.
- The average support payment is only 13 percent of the father's income.
- Only 48 percent of dads who are ordered to pay child support do so regularly. Twenty-seven percent pay partially; 26 percent never pay.
- Twenty percent of parents are not in complete compliance when child-support agreements were voluntarily agreed to.
- Fewer than 10 percent of divorce settlements include college tuition.

It is illegal for a parent not to pay court-ordered support. The Supreme Court has upheld nonpayment as civil contempt, which means a parent who has failed to pay may be jailed. This is a powerful remedy against self-employed parents and those who are able to hide assets, especially in cases where a state can't reach a parent by withholding wages. Child-support legislation currently under consideration would make income withholding automatic, rather than waiting for a parent to default. But for now, withholding of wages of parents deliquent in making child-support payments is the primary remedy and is becoming increasingly available. It is important to take action when your ex first defaults, before payments accumulate. Being generous, forgiving, and patient seldom work to your benefit. Anything that involves the legal system is slow, so it is important not to wait long before taking action.

And there are places for you to turn for help. Among these are state agencies such as CSEA (Child Support

Enforcement Administration), the Legal Aid Society, legal clinics, the IRS Interceptor Program, or your attorney. Another helpful tool is the booklet, "Child Support: Methods of Collecting Everything You're Entitled To." It will take you by the hand and lead

---

Uncle Sam to Your Rescue

The Federal Child Support Enforcement Amendments of 1984 require employers, when directed by the appropriate state agency, to automatically withhold child support from the wages of employees who are more than 30 days delinquent in their payments. States may also collect from other sources such as tax refunds and bank accounts.

Send for a free copy of the "Handbook on Child Support Enforcement," a 40-page booklet that lists the basic steps to follow if you need child-support enforcement services, plus tips on solving enforcement problems:

> Consumer Information Center
> Box 100, Department CS
> Pueblo, CO 81009

or contact:

> Office of Child Support Enforcement
>   and Reference Center.
> US Dept. of Health and Human Services
> 5th floor
> 370 L'Enfant Promenade, S.W.
> Washington, DC 20047
> (202) 252-5431
> This center also publishes a national newsletter and provides other informative booklets.

For rights of military spouses, contact:

> EXPOSE
> PO Box 11191
> Alexandria, VA 22312
> (703)941-5844

you through the necessary steps as well as provide you with the worksheets you will need to proceed. For a copy send $7 to Resources, PO Box 5019, 155 East C St., Upland, CA 91786.

You can also get the emotional support you will be needing at this juncture by joining your local chapter of ACES (Association for Children for Enforcement of Support). For information on a chapter in your state (or how to establish one) contact, ACES, 1018 Jefferson Ave., #204, Toledo, OH 43624.

Another group you may wish to contact is the National Council for Children's Rights, Inc. (NCCR), 2001 O Street NW, Washington, DC, 20036 (202)223-6227, which lobbies nationally on behalf of parents regarding the divorce and support laws that affect them. The NCCR publishes reports, audiocassettes, model bills, legal briefs, and information about school-based programs to help children of separation and divorce.

Despite the grim picture painted here, keep in mind that hundreds of thousands of divorced, noncustodial parents are financially responsible.

MAKING IT LEGAL

Divorce is a legal dissolution of marriage, and the laws that cover it are different in every state. In even the most amicable of divorces, you'll need a lawyer to lead you through the legal ramifications. You never understand the legality of your marriage until it comes to taking it apart in a divorce. If you had no children, you could use a do-it-yourself kit. But you do have children, so you need to be sure their interests are protected, too.

Today, no-fault divorce means it is not necessary to do an autopsy on a marriage to place blame for its failure. Beware of conducting your own ongoing dissection of your marital split. If the marriage is over—even if for only one spouse—then it is over for both.

Mediation As an Option

When disassembling a marriage—a life—a family needs all the resources it can muster. Professional help *is* available for you. In my opinion, one type of help—mediation—should be practically mandatory in every divorce, especially when there are differences of opinion about custody and money. Mediators are not there to take sides or to try to save a marriage, or to decide issues. They help a couple to define the issues and reach agreement. They operate on the premise that the parents' divorce is not the end of the family, but the beginning of the reorganization of the family into two separate units—an idea distinctly comforting to children. After general agreement is reached with a mediator, it is still necessary to see a lawyer to implement the terms of the divorce.

Private mediation is a service that is less expensive than your legal fees will probably prove to be. Trained third parties bring you together into an emotionally safe environment to help you bring your divorce to its legal conclusion. Mediation is NOT a binding decision by a third party; mediators do not try to act as divorce lawyers. They will help the two of you work out an agreement that you take to your lawyers for its legal conclusion. Mediators can deal with your finances, your custody and visitation schedules, and anything else you need help negotiating. A good mediator will

---

It's better to send your own kids to college than your lawyer's.

—*Stephen Erickson, J.D., mediator*

keep you focused on the task and help you arrive at what you both think is fair.

Even if you "drop out," most people feel mediation is worthwhile because many, if not all, of your issues can be decided on or at least discussed. One problem with mediation is that the "weaker personality" or the person hurting the most might not be able to stand up for his or her needs at this difficult time. Skilled mediators can balance the process. In addition, any conclusions must be reviewed by the lawyers for each party so each person is protected. And mediation settlements often prove more successful than court-settled cases. It seems that when both parties participate in the decision, both usually fulfill their part of the agreement. According to Hugh McIssac, director of the Los Angeles Conciliation Court's Services, "Recent research shows that kids do best when parents have reached a mediated settlement."

You can mediate custody, money matters, or any issue of concern. Or you may choose to mediate just one of the matters. Because both parents are interested in having the needs of the children met, mediation is often used in this area. In many states mediation is mandatory if parents are unable to reach an agreement in court.

Divorce researcher Judith Wallerstein has been critical of the treatment of children in mediation. For example, in a mediated case where a couple agreed that their two sons would live for a full year with each parent during alternate years, no one observed the sons or inquired whether it appeared that the children could make this kind of adjustment. "It may well be that the mediated settlement was in the best interests of these children, but there is no evidence that their needs were considered," commented Wallerstein. "Children are infrequently seen by mediators."

Consider letting your children participate in at least

one of your sessions, if you are not locked in battle. It
will allay their fears about what is going on and will
give them a chance to speak, be heard, and thereby
gain a sense of control over their lives. My children
were surprised at the orderliness of mediation. They
had envisioned a long table where we sparred verbally
with mediators trying to control us. They were surprised about the small room, the informal setting, and
the fact that the mediator was in charge.

---

*Before going to custody mediation services provided by
our local county court service, we used the book, MOM'S
HOUSE—DAD'S HOUSE as our guideline. It helped
tremendously—again by putting the focus on our parenting roles rather than on our differences.*
—Karyn Herrmann, Minneapolis, MN

You can use mediation after your divorce is final,
too. The process can be helpful in discussing changes
in visitation and other child-oriented concerns. In fact,
you might want a clause in your divorce decree requiring that you first use mediation to modify the existing
agreement before legal action can be taken.

Arbitration

Another kind of help is arbitration. Although used
infrequently in settling a divorce with the growing use
of mediation, in some cases, when no solution seems
possible, it can save divorcing couples the expense
and turmoil of a court battle. More often it is used to
settle subsequent disputes that might arise out of a
divorce decree when arbitration has been specified as
the solution for future changes. Arbitration tends to be
used most frequently in property divisions. It can be

Divorce Mediation and Counseling Sources

The Academy of Family Mediators
PO Box 10501
Eugene OR 97440
(503)345-1205

American Bar Association Dispute Resolution
Center
1800 M St. NW
Washington, DC 20036
(202)331-2258

Association of Family and Conciliation Courts
Oregon Health Sciences University,
Dept. of Psychiatry
3181 SW Sam Jackson Park Rd.
Portland, OR 97201
(503)279-5651

Family Mediation Association
9308 Bulls Run Pkwy.
Bethesda, MD 20817
(301)654-7708
Provides directory of FMA-certified mediators
throughout the United States.

Family Service Associations of America
11700 W. Lake Park Drive
Milwaukee, WI 53224
(414)359-2111
Provides information about U.S. agencies offering divorce counseling.

The Christian Legal Society
PO Box 1492
Merrifield, VA 22116
(703)560-7314

used for only a part of your divorce settlement, rather than the whole configuration of issues.

The arbitrator is a person hired and empowered to judge a case and make decisions. Arbitration hearings work like courts but are more informal. Affidavits aren't required and witnesses are not expected to be advocates for either side. In binding arbitration, the spouses agree beforehand that they will abide by the arbitrator's decision. In advisory, nonbinding arbitration, the parties may reject a decision, and the case can still go to court. Even when an agreement hasn't been reached, both parties often emerge from this process better prepared to settle their case.

For more information, contact The American Arbitration Association, 140 W. 51st Street, New York, NY 10020, (212)484-4000. They will also direct you to local arbitration associations. They make available a pamphlet with AAA rules and addresses of 24 regional offices.

Your Lawyer

There is your emotional divorce and there is your legal divorce. The first you must do yourself. The second you can't do without a lawyer. If you haven't contacted a lawyer by now—and you are separated—you have little choice but to line one up for yourself immediately. You will need to find someone familiar with family law and comfortable handling divorce cases.

Your lawyer will need to know what you want—if you know—in settling your divorce. You will need to consider your house, your money, assets, and debts, custody of your children, and your future. It will be necessary to provide information about your finances and those of your spouse.

Most people begin the legal part of their divorce with naive, preset ideas. Women tend to be either

angry ("I'll get him for all he's worth" attitude) or the
reverse—a passive ("Let's not get him upset" attitude).
Men, on the other hand, tend to assume that the divorce can be done quickly, the assets divided fairly
(which is usually their definition of "fair") with any
business assets going to them, selling the house, and
seeing the kids whenever they think they should or
can. None of these scenarios are common. The legal
process usually takes on a life and time frame of its
own over which neither party exerts control. This is
often one of the biggest surprises about divorcing to
men and women alike.

What Will the Lawyer Do?

You can expect your lawyer to do the following:

- File your suit for divorce, see that the papers are
  served on your spouse, and handle the slew of legal
  documents the procedure requires.
- Provide you with advice on your rights and review
  decisions made between you and your spouse.
- Review any agreements you arrive at through a mediator to be sure they are legal and not unfair to you.
- Negotiate with your spouse through his or her law-
  yer(s) if you cannot reach agreement about the division of property, alimony, and/or child-support
  settlements and custody arrangements. (It is not
  standard operating procedure for one spouse to talk
  to the other's lawyer.) This unfortunately makes the
  process more expensive for all involved. However,
  there is no prohibition about you and your spouse
  talking; but do discuss this first with your lawyer
  before you take it upon yourself to enter into direct
  negotiations.
- Represent you in court if negotiations are not
  successful.

What your lawyer will NOT do is act as a peacemaker for you. If your spouse assaults you, do not call your lawyer until after you have called the police and pressed charges. Neither lawyers nor judges can help you handle visitation problems. Do not waste your money by calling your lawyer with "She's turning the kids against me" or "He never picks the kids up on time" problems. Your lawyer might like to help you but there is nothing he or she can actually do.

Be aware that a lawyer, especially an adversarial lawyer, may aggravate your difficulties with your spouse. Your lawyer is your advocate, and if he or she is aggressive, this may create problems years from now when you must still have contact with your ex. Keep in mind that lawyers also tend to represent the perceived best interests of parents, not those of the children.

NEVER NEGOTIATE A SIDE DEAL WITH YOUR EXITING SPOUSE OR SIGN ANYTHING WITHOUT TALKING TO YOUR LAWYER FIRST.

Watching my lawyer, my spouse's lawyer, and the judge in our first confrontation in a court hearing was eye-opening for me. I realized that there was a language, a protocol, a ritual occurring that had little to do with our case but completely impacted on it. I then understood why you don't represent yourself in court. It had little to do with truth or fairness. Lawyers know the game that is being played and that's what you are paying for.

—Tammi Green, Chelsea, MI

Choosing a Lawyer

Referrals from friends and business acquaintances are the most common way to find local lawyers. You can also phone your local Bar Association for referrals, or find lawyers listed under "Attorneys" in the Yellow Pages. Some states have certified specialty laws, which require that lawyers demonstrate a level of competence in a given field before they can specialize. There is also an American Academy of Matrimonial Lawyers that you can contact for referrals (20 N. Michigan Ave., Chicago, IL 60602, 312-263-6477). Many states offer free legal aid, but you'll probably have to put your name on a waiting list; if it is determined that your income is too large, however, you will not qualify for the service.

Ask for an appointment to interview your prospective lawyer. Make it clear to this lawyer in your telephone call that you want this initial meeting as an interview *only*. There should be no charge for a half-hour consultation. Interview at least three lawyers, if time permits. You will learn a lot in the process both about the lawyer, your case, and how you interact with your prospective lawyer. You should feel a rapport and trust with your lawyer. In an interview:

- Try to get a reading on how each lawyer feels about divorce, joint custody, and mediation.
- Find out what percentage of his or her time is spent on divorce clients. How long has he or she been practicing family law? You want a lawyer who knows your local court personnel and procedures and has frequent contact with the judicial officers who will be hearing your case, if you think that you might end up in court.
- Inquire as to what the monetary range is for cases similar to yours.
- Ask about fees and billing procedures. There are flat fees, percentage of property settlement fees (illegal in some states), and hourly fees. Many ask for an opening retainer (deposit). You will be billed

also for phone calls, correspondence, time spent in court, and time conversing with the opposing lawyer.

• Ask if there will (or can) be a written agreement that will cover what your charges will be, the way you will be billed, and what the lawyer will and will not do. (This should be signed by you and your lawyer when you do hire one.)

Don't share a lawyer with your spouse. It may seem less expensive but in the long run it almost surely will not be. It's also illegal in some states.

Until recently, lawyers have tended to frown upon the use of mediation—whether because of concern for their clients, fear of potential loss of clients, or just unfamiliarity with the concept. But as attorneys are becoming more familiar with its use as well as being exposed to it in law school, mediation is becoming more widespread. Time lost with one client, they are realizing, has translated into more time for additional clients.

Money-Saving Tips

It has been said that some lawyers prolong proceedings to earn more money. This is true, but there is no real way of determining it. You must remember to maintain some sort of control as you proceed, even asking for an occasional recap on where your case is going. Making this judgment call is difficult, because you only get one chance to determine how you will live for a long time and you must do the best you can for yourself.

You will learn to measure your words in terms of time because time is costly with lawyers. *Don't* use your lawyer as your therapist. It might feel good to have a lawyer who is a good listener but it will also be expensive. It's less expensive and more effective to go

to a therapist to deal with the emotional unfairness of
your divorce. Also:

- Learn to use your lawyer's secretary effectively. Call
  to relay information or confirm correspondence without having to speak to your lawyer.
- Write rather than call. Conversations can be longer
  than you planned, especially if you are doing a lot
  of talking or your lawyer is content to do a lot of
  listening.
- Don't call to complain about your spouse. Do so
  only when calling can accomplish something.
- When you do call, make a list of what you want to
  discuss beforehand, so your comments and questions will be specific.

Remember, you are the one who has hired the lawyer. Your lawyer works for you. It's never easy to
know when to accept or reject advice given you. You're
going to have to live with your divorce decree—not
your lawyer or your friends. You may make mistakes
in this area that only time will reveal. Your advocate
will be trying to look down the road for you but will
never walk in your shoes. There is no shame in changing lawyers at any point in the proceedings if you feel
your interests will be better served by a change in
attorneys. If you do discharge your attorney, however,
do it in writing and keep a copy of your dated letter.

You should expect to pay your own attorney's fees,
even if you did not initiate the divorce. That's the
usual procedure today. If payment is a problem, most
lawyers will be willing to work out a monthly payment plan.

Try to keep things in perspective when problems
arise. There is probably not a lot a lawyer can do at 9
P.M. on a Sunday other than get irritated. Although it

may be rough on you at times, remember that lawyers are people, too.

There is no such thing as a win or victory in settling your divorce. The end result will be a shade of gray, not black or white. If you can both walk away feeling only somewhat dissatisfied, then it was probably a fair outcome.

During our negotiation proceedings my husband was doing some unfair, even illegal, actions. I could afford to fight him. A male friend gave me some important insights. He said, based on my tiresome retelling of my "poor me" story, "It sounds like your husband has to win to be a whole person—do you?" That helped me take a step back and look at what was really happening. I directed my lawyers to settle, against their advice. The bottom line worked out okay, though never the 50–50 that I was due, but I saved myself incredible additional heartache. My ex continued to indicate he was shortchanged. Yet I now know that if he had not felt he had "won," I'd probably still be fighting for my half today.
—Toni Mitchell, Mt. Vernon, NY

Going to Court for Custody

Going to court to have custody determined is probably the hardest thing any family will have to face. A stranger (even if he or she is a kindly-looking judge), will probably take no more than five minutes of deliberation to decide your family's fate for years to come. And one parent will come away feeling like a loser. If you think a court battle in which the children are the prize becomes "proof" that you are the more loving parent, guess again. It's a self-deception. It's also a rotten thing to do to your kids. In a custody battle, they are no longer your children but fought-over possessions; and they know it—and may even use it to play you and your ex-spouse off against each other.

If your children are asked for their preference (which usually happens with early teens), they are given power that perhaps they should not have. No matter what, they will be settling for second best because they will prefer their first choice of having both parents together. Asking their choice of parent and living arrangements puts incredible pressure on children, because they must hurt one parent terribly. Often they have to convince themselves that the parent they rejected is really bad in order to justify having made a preference choice. Neither parent nor (hopefully) the judge will directly ask children who they wish to live with. To do so will damage any parent-child relationship. The best thing to hope for is that the judge will render the least harmful judgment. But don't kid yourself; it will not be easy on anyone involved.

If children are involved by the judge, the interview will be conducted in private in the judge's chambers. This is called an "in camera" ("in chambers") proceeding. It will be attended by the children and the lawyers. Many courts have court-appointed social workers interview both parents and children beforehand for an assessment of the situation. If the custody fight is really ugly, the court might even appoint an attorney for the children to protect their rights.

If your children will be involved in your legalities, be sure to talk with them about the reason this is happening, stressing that it is not their fault and acknowledging that it is not an easy situation for them. Don't discuss what they should say to a judge even though they might want some idea about what will be asked of them.

If the judgment has gone against you, your children should know that it hasn't changed your love for them. A judge can decide whether your kids will live with you or not, but not how much you love them. Let them know your commitment to them wasn't based on "winning" in court. Be honest without being divisive. You can express sadness, but tell them you all will make this work as best you can.

Keep in mind that going to court for a property settlement or custody case always costs more than you thought and will be painfully lengthy, keeping your life on hold.

When I was going through a custody battle the judge complimented my ex-wife and me for never downgrading the other parent to the child. I felt so "clean" about that and even better that the custody battle ended. The emphasis is now on cooperation.

—David Levy, Washington, DC

The judge can decide whether your kids will live with you but not how much you'll love them. Just keep loving them, whatever happens, and they'll know in their hearts they can count on you.

—16-year-old daughter, now living with the noncustodial mother

---

Custody of children can change if circumstances change. It's best when these changes can be done without going to court.

WHEN YOU ARE GETTING KICKED FROM BEHIND, IT MEANS YOU'RE OUT IN FRONT.

CUSTODY

I did not save custody as the last issue to discuss because it is less important, but rather because it is the

---

IN SUMMATION—LEGAL GUIDES

You can save yourself some dollars and get a greater sense of what you must face if you do a little reading on your own. Check out your bookstore or library for titles such as these:

THE DIVORCE HANDBOOK: YOUR BASIC GUIDE TO DIVORCE
by J. T. Friedman
(Random House, 1984)

THE COMPLETE LEGAL GUIDE TO MARRIAGE, DIVORCE, CUSTODY AND LIVING TOGETHER
by S. M. Sack
(McGraw-Hill, 1987)

THE DIVORCE LAW HANDBOOK
by E. D. Samuelson
(Human Sciences Press, 1988)

*See page 243.

MOST important. Custody is the arrangement we work out to participate in our legal responsibility for our children.

CUSTODY IS ACCESS TO OUR CHILDREN. CUSTODY IS ALSO CHILDREN'S ACCESS TO THEIR PARENTS.

Instead of fighting over which parent gets custody—making the children a battleground for your divorce—the focus should be placed on WHEN each child will be with you.

Legal custody (sole, joint, or otherwise) does not necessarily have to reflect how your custodial (physical custody) relationship actually works. In some families the legal sole custodian is one parent, while the children still split their time fairly evenly between the two parents. And there is legal joint custody where a father's visitation schedule may actually be minimal. Legal sole custody means only that one parent is given the authority to make medical, religious, educational, and legal decisions for the child without having to consult or inform the other parent. Joint legal custody means you are both responsible for sharing in these decisions. In reality, even in a joint custody situation, these decisions may fall by habit or circumstance to one parent. In short, the terms *joint legal* and *joint physical* are often used interchangeably today as *joint custody.* But joint custody will translate differently for each family. It's an umbrella term that can describe many different arrangements. Joint custody doesn't mean equal but it tends to indicate a flexible or equitable approach to parenting.

Figuring out how you will arrange your custody situation is obviously an important part of separating and divorcing. It will determine the boundaries of the joys and benefits of being a parent, as well as limit a child's right to be parented by both parents. It has financial implications (e.g., "Will I get less if he or she sees them more often?") and perhaps more important, emotional complications (e.g., "Will his/her new 'significant other' replace me as my children's father/mother?"). For many parents, children will be the providers of love, companionship, and even purpose, which causes them to become the focal point of a custody battle. These are understandable parental needs—but they should not be filled at the expense of a child's emotional health. The best interest of a child is *never* served by being the focal point of any battle.

GOOD PARENTAL ATTITUDES AND
COOPERATION, RATHER THAN ANY
SPECIFIC CUSTODIAL ARRANGEMENTS
YOU MAKE, WILL ULTIMATELY
HELP YOUR CHILD MAKE HIS
OR HER BEST ADJUSTMENT.

Interwoven in your custodial arrangement is *visitation*, also known as *access*. Visitation/access is an artificial and arbitrary concept that enables the court to keep peace between the parents by specifying dates and times of contact. It's also insurance that a noncustodial parent has access to his or her children. This is an important concept because children need and are entitled to both parents. And the freer the access a child has to both, the better it usually is for the child. Today many states even recognize the validity of grandparents' rights to visitation.

The term *reasonable visitation*, included in many custody agreements, is a broad and indefinite concept, if one is left with just those words. "Reasonable" refers to what's best for the children first, and for the parents, second. It allows for a variety of visiting patterns that may range from almost daily, if the children are very young, to annually, if the parents live far apart. "Reasonable" should always be translated into a minimum of specific dates and days in any custody agreement. The word *custody* has the unfortunate overtone of ownership and some states are choosing to eliminate the use of the word. It has been suggested that even the words *access* or *visitation* be replaced with *family time* or *parenting time*, and *noncustodial parent* with *nonresidential parent*. To any parent with inadequate time with his or her children, any and all of these terms are reprehensible.

Dr. Maria Isaacs, psychologist and director of the Families of Divorce Project in Philadelphia, has reported that the impact of a stable visitation arrangement is more positive than the frequency of visits. Fathers with visitation schedules see their children more often than ones without a schedule. Most important, children who have regular visitation arrangements for up to three years after their parents' separation do best and are more competent socially. Families who had established schedules in the first year of separation were most likely to maintain them, indicating that the first year is a crucial period to set future patterns.

When parents live in the same area, perhaps the most common arrangement is a weekly visit, which may or may not include an overnight stay. It may take awhile for visiting routines that work best for all to be worked out. Parents can always enlarge upon and vary any arrangements initially made.

Parents shouldn't be considered visitors when their children are with them, even if it's only once a week. Words can have powerful meaning, and the term visitation creates negative images about the relationship between non-custodial parents and their children.
  —*David Levy, Esq., President*
  National Council for Children's Rights, Inc.,
  Washington, DC

No matter how your custody arrangement works at first, it is likely to change over the years and have to be renegotiated or rearranged. Although difficult, renegotiation may be easier further down the road because you have settled other matters and have built some trust, history, and expectations about your former spouse in the area of parenting.

What Are the Options in Custody?

Sole custody, when given, is almost invariably held by the mother. But this is changing rapidly, as noncustodial fathers become more vocal and more women enter the work force. Over a hundred years ago, fathers always got custody "because children (and wives) were considered chattel." Our current stereotyped ideas of the mother as best nurturer are changing, too. Just as we realize that either parent may be able to supply the nurturing, supportive atmosphere kids need, we have devised many arrangements that allow parents to work out the details of custody in ways that will be best for all. California, which has always been a leader in matters of family law, enacted a Joint Custody provision in divorce laws a number of years ago. By 1986, 33 states had followed suit and in 13 of those states it is the preferred option. Courts are free to order *joint custody* now, even if one parent opposes it.

Some states distinguish between "legal" joint custody, in which parents have equal rights in decision making, and "physical" joint custody (also referred to by some as split custody, just to add to the confusion), in which children live with each parent for equitable (meaning not necessarily equal) or equal amounts of time. According to the NCCR, the minimum amount of time that generally qualifies as physical joint custody is at least one-third of the time with either parent in a legal joint custodial agreement. In a joint physical custody arrangement, most parents prefer the terms *co-parenting, shared parenting,* or *separate parenting.* One joint custody alternative that has received some publicity is called the "birds' nest" arrangement. The family home is kept intact for the kids, and the parents move in and out on a regular schedule. This arrangement can work initially, but it usually doesn't succeed over any period of time—and the expense of maintaining three domiciles is prohibitive.

Other kinds of custody besides sole or joint are possible, and special circumstances may make one or another more desirable:

- *Alternating custody.* A child lives with one parent for a fairly lengthy period—perhaps a year or more—then with the other. This arrangement sometimes is a solution when the parents are separated by great geographic distance.
- *Split custody.* Each parent has sole custody of one or more of the children. Courts seldom divide children, believing that siblings should grow up together and that older children can help younger ones adjust to the new way of life. Yet, for some families this works best. For example, a teenage son may live with his father, whereas younger siblings stay with the mother.
- *Serial custody.* One parent has custody of the children for several years, and then the other. A father, for example, may take over the custody of teenage boys if a mother finds she cannot handle them or if both parents agree they need to be with a male.
- *Third-party custody.* This is where custody is sought by a grandparent, another family member, a non-family member, or the state. Child neglect or abuse are usually the reasons for the court to conclude that a parent should not have custody of a child.

Parents who jointly make custody decisions about their children are the parents who, fortunately, feel the least amount of "unfairness," and for whom custodial arrangements work best. Court decisions about custody are necessary only when parents can't agree. Anything that both parents want to arrange or experiment with can be done even after all the papers are signed without involving lawyers and judges. Changes in divorce decrees for legal purposes are another matter.

In the throes of divorce, foresight dims. To fight over how many weekends or vacations your children will spend with your ex is foolish and to everyone's detriment. Kids love change and you'll discover that child-free weekends are so great that they might have even saved your marriage.
—Hester Mundis, W. Shokan, NY

The best custody arrangement for your family will be the one that takes into consideration the needs of both parents and children. Be imaginative. There are many options.

Who Decides?

Custody decisions are often made when tempers are the hottest. They are not always in the best interest of all concerned. Custody and visitation should be flexible enough to meet the changing desires and needs of all the people involved.

In about 75 percent of divorce cases, parents themselves make custody decisions, often with the help of mediators. Some resort to arbitration. For the others—10 to 15 percent—there are legal custody battles that can be expensive, impersonal, and painful.

Let the Children Choose?

It's unfair for parents to force children to take sides by even casually asking them their preferences in custody matters. Too often children choose one parent over another out of loyalty for the one they perceive as "wronged" or because they think one needs them more than the other does. Whatever they say, children struggle with guilt and fairness issues. Often what we ask when we ask our children this question really is, "Who do you love more? Mommy or Daddy?" This is no different than the question children with siblings often ask, "Don't you really love me more than Susie?" Yes, we all love to be anyone's favorite person, especially a significant family member's. It's a normal fantasy. But it's a childish question or hope at best. Divorcing spouses too often look upon their children as possessions to be fought over instead of as individuals whose interests should come first. Financial problems, insecurity, visitation terms, and just plain anger often cause parents to use their children as pawns without realizing they are doing that. Few, if any, would consciously put their children in the middle, but they fail to see that is exactly what is happening as they deal with their own emotional agendas. Parents are wise to consider any definite wishes that are expressed, but final decisions should be made by the parents—and the children should know that.

Custody Problems

As difficult as this whole custody issue is, for many it becomes even more problematic. Adults lose sight of their children's needs as they escalate actions that use the children as their pawns—and may lead to manipulation by the children.

Denied Access/Visitation

Unfortunate but true: A 1977 study by the National Institutes of Health reports that during the first two years after divorce, 40 percent of those custodial mothers asked admitted that they had, at least once, refused to let their ex-husbands see their children for punitive reasons. It's important to remember that you can't use visitation as a weapon, or means of making a statement about your ex's parenting skills ("Our child is watching too much TV at your house") or to express disapproval of your former spouse's new "significant other." It is not acceptable to deny access to punish a spouse who left you for another. This sort of revenge will hurt your child more than your ex. However, access to children for abusive, violent, noncustodial parents needs to be limited and conditional (i.e., requiring the presence of a third party, and such).

If you are worried, as the noncustodial parent, that access may become a problem, keep a diary or log of events to prove visitation has been denied. And if you know anyone who has witnessed your access being denied, ask them if they will verify that if the need arises. Don't withhold support payments, because you'll only weaken your own case. Before seeking legal help, send a registered letter (and keep a copy) in which you request, in nonthreatening words, a return of your visitation schedule so that you won't be forced to seek any enforcement of your rights.

I was divorced when my daughter was two and a half. She's eleven now. Our custody arrangements looked great on paper but my ex-husband decided not to abide by them and chose his own arrangements instead. He calls once a year at Christmas and demands to see her. I don't comply and he thinks I'm unreasonable. And he doesn't see how unfair he is being to our daughter.
—Kathi Baldwin, Rancho Cucamongo, CA

The legal remedies for denied visitation are expensive. A writ of habeas corpus can compel a custodial parent who has denied visitation to appear in court. The parent can be cited for contempt or even be punished by temporary cessation of all or part of support payments. If your custodial ex-spouse has made an

unwarranted move out of state, then you can trigger
the Uniform Child Custody Jurisdiction Act, which
has been adopted by all 50 states. Your visitation can
be enforced even if your child is halfway across the
country. Some states now have laws making even a
late return of a child visiting a noncustodial parent a
felony.

A court cannot force a parent to act responsibly as a
father or mother against his or her will. A parent who
refuses to visit at allocated times and is current on any
financial obligations will be beyond the reach of the
law.

The Accusing Finger

Custody and visitation may be denied legally if a
parent can be shown to be abusive—physically or sexually. Defending against this accusation is no easy
matter. There are numerous cases today where sexual
and spousal abuse are being brought (some believe) to
keep noncustodial fathers or mothers from their children. Molestation litigation has been referred to by
one author as "the nuclear bomb of custody hearing."
True or false, these charges are painful for all involved. Polygraph testing is now being suggested as
one way to deal with this problem. Each parent would
be tested, as well as the child. And children can ma-
nipulate such a situation as well as an angry parent.

According to Dr. Melvin Greyer of Family Law Project of the University of Michigan, most sexual abuse
allegations made in custody disputes are false. Mothers are also much more likely to make these allegations than fathers. In his study of 30 cases of alleged
sexual abuse, 83 percent were unconfirmed.

Self-help support groups have formed to counter
these false charges. You can contact Victims of Child
Abuse Laws (VOCAL), a self-help group for people

falsely accused of child sexual abuse during a custody suit. Write to VOCAL, Box 11335, Minneapolis, MN 55411 (612-521-9714) for more information. Or contact the National Congress for Men (NCM), 223 15th St. SE, Washington, DC 20003 (202-FATHERS), which will supply you with a comprehensive list of support groups for a small fee. They will also direct you to help in areas of special problems, including lawyer referrals.

Parental Kidnapping

Thousands of children are spirited away from their homes by noncustodial parents every year. Most child snatching occurs right before or after divorce proceedings. This parental kidnapping has been described as the last desperate act in the tragic ending of a relationship. In many cases, the primary motivation is not concern for the child. Rather, spite and a desire to get even and shut the other parent out of the child's life are the motivations, although the angry parent is often unaware of this. Parental kidnapping is a federal offense.

According to Mary Anne Kiser, founder of Parents Alone, in Wichita, Kansas, abductions by an estranged parent can be predicted in 75 percent of the cases. Parents' perceptions and fear of abduction are often valid indicators. A history of violence is another link, including threats to kill the custodial parent. Fifty-three percent of abductors had beaten their spouses and 30 percent had beaten a firstborn child. Children ages 3 to 9 are the most vulnerable to abduction. Age, not sex, is the main factor.

Still, there is little legal protection available beforehand. A parent's visitation rights usually will not be curtailed unless there is serious harm, or the likelihood of kidnapping can be proven. Every state now has adopted the Federal Uniform Child Custody Jurisdiction Act, however, which honors and enforces custody and visitation decisions made in another state. This means you can obtain an enforcement order in your state and it is given full force and effect in your ex's state.

Although it is a crime to kidnap your child by taking him or her to a different state, a parent taking a child out of the country will effectively circumvent American law in most cases. There are no legal recourses for a parent. No international agreements specifically cover custody cases. The greatest number of children taken out of the United States are taken to West Germany, Mexico, the United Kingdom, and Italy. Those taken to the Middle East are the hardest to recover, because of cultural differences where women have little clout and the fact that foreign citizen fathers can get passports of their country for their children.

Being Cautious

Always take an angry spouse's threats of abduction seriously. Generally child snatchers do not keep their intentions a secret. Here are a few precautions to take if you fear kidnapping by your noncustodial spouse:

- Stay on good terms with your ex-spouse, as well as with his or her family and friends. Most child snatchings are undertaken to get revenge.
- Compile a *trail* file for tracing your spouse: social security number, driver's license, credit card numbers, and maybe even bank account numbers.
- Advise school personnel about your concerns and tell them to allow only someone you have delegated to take your child from the school grounds.
- Ask teachers, bus drivers, and others who are likely to be on school grounds to watch for suspicious

loiterers who appear to be interested in your child and to notify you of them.
- Prepare your child without alarming him or her. If you have sole custody, let your child know he or she does not have the right to go anywhere without your permission—even with the other parent.
- Write the U.S. Passport Office and request that no passport be issued to a child of yours on application of the other parent. You will need to enclose a certified copy of the court order of legal custody.
- Alert local police to your fears so they will respond immediately to a call from you. They may require a certified copy of your custody order.

Missing Children Organizations

Child-Find, for a fee, will help publicize your child's disappearance:
PO Box 277
New Paltz, NY 12561
1-800-I AM LOST

Another organization that has successfully conducted searches for missing children is the
National Center for Missing and Exploited Children
1835 K St. NW #600
Washington, DC 20006
(202)634-9821 or 1-800-843-5678

Missing Children Network
300 Orchard City Drive
Campbell, CA 95008
1-800-235-3535

6

Sole Custody and the
Noncustodial Parent

Sole legal and physical custody is still common today, and many legal joint custody situations resemble sole custodial arrangements. Some parents seek sole custody because they think it shows the world who is the better, more devoted parent. Others erroneously pursue sole custody, thinking they will never have to deal with that "other" parent again. Both are a gross misunderstanding of sole custody. Sometimes it's the best choice; sometimes it simply happens when a parent leaves the family. Sole custody means that one parent will provide most of the day-to-day care for the children. It does not mean, or have to mean, solo parenting.

Many people still feel that mother-custody is more appropriate. The Committee for Mother and Child Rights in Chappaqua, New York, believes that mothers should have first rights in custody decisions because they bear the children and almost always play a larger nurturing role in their children's lives than do fathers. In order to minimize a child's confusion, conventional wisdom has previously stressed one home and one primary caretaker. This has traditionally fallen to the mother. But sole custody is not easy on mothers. With the children and total child-care responsibilities often comes financial insecurity, loss of one's identity as an

142

adult who is part of a couple, anger at being left (if that is the case), possible loss of a home, and probably entry (or reentry) into the job market during a period of life when rewarding jobs are hard to come by.

WHO IS THE BETTER PARENT? THERE IS NO ANSWER TO SUCH A QUESTION. IF YOU THINK THERE IS, BE ASSURED IT IS PROBABLY NOT YOU.

Custodial parents often come to believe that they alone are the *real* parent. This is never more than half true! The world is changing. Fathers who have been active in the birthing, diapering, and feeding of their children are no longer quietly going along with the conventional mother-custody tradition. Rather than lose custody, many fathers are actively seeking it. In the process, the needs of the children are seldom seen in an unemotional light.

I had sole custody. It was a very hefty, total responsibility. I had no vacation time until she was old enough for sleep-away camp.
—Susan Resnik, New York City

SINGLE-FATHER HOUSEHOLDS

According to the Census Bureau some 893,000 fathers head single-parent families today, rearing more than one million children. No more than 10 percent of these are widowers. These single fathers are discover-

ing what single custodial mothers have known for a
long time—raising kids while trying to make a living
is incredibly hard work!

Should custody be a gender-related decision? No.
It's important to look realistically at what each parent
can offer practically and emotionally and what children need at each point in their lives. There are many
fathers who make and have made good primary care-
takers. Fathers approach the parenting jobs much the
same way that mothers do. Custodial fathers provide
about the same amount of hugs, well-balanced meals,
and piano lessons as custodial mothers.

Are You Really Ready for Sole Custody?

- Are you good at juggling schedules?
- Do you have the management skills necessary to
  run a home for two or more?
- Can you be happy owning a family car or van?
- Can you feel comfortable teaching your son and/or
  daughter about sex?
- How will your staying home with a sick child
  affect your job?
- Can you provide the appropriate role model when
  it comes to dating and social life?
- Can you handle the kind of criticism and emotional ups and downs that kids bring to a relationship? (And you thought living with your
  ex-spouse was hard!)

Although more fathers are now willing to ask for
custody, roughly half of custodial fathers get custody
by default, with only 20 percent winning custody in
court battles. Some women feel that their ex-husbands
seek sole custody to avoid child-support payments,
feeling that it's "cheaper" to care for the children
themselves, and that sole custody gives them more

control. Because men usually have a more stable financial footing, they are becoming equal contenders in such battles. In his book, *Single Fathers*, Jeffrey Grief reports that single fathers have an easier time rearing younger children. But because they believe they can't take care of younger children, many fathers don't seek custody.

I was divorced when my boys were seven and a half and ten and a half. They see their dad half of the summer, half of Christmas vacation, and at Easter. He lives in another part of the state. One of my boys romanticized the freedom there so much that we let him live there for a year and a half. He returned with the conclusion that all that "freedom" (lack of supervision) didn't make him feel loved. They know that when they get older they can live with him if they choose.

—Barbara Wade, Napa, CA

One interesting footnote. Children whose fathers have custody also have more frequent contact with the noncustodial mother than do their counterparts in homes where the mother has sole custody.

NONCUSTODIAL MOTHERS

More than one million mothers in the United States do not have physical custody of their children. Apparently half of these mothers become noncustodial by choice, believing that the father is a good parent and can offer a more secure home. Whatever the circumstances, even today these women must cope with a certain amount of social stigma. Society seems to penalize them for not being the custodial parent. They're often labeled "runaway" or "absentee" mothers. Most women who do not want physical custody are subject to a lot of peer and family pressure. These women often do not publicly admit to their noncustodial status. They have to deal with the questions: "What did you do to lose custody?" or "What kind of a mother would choose to give up her kids?" Ironically, single-father support group meetings are among the few places where they can find understanding and help.

FOR MOTHERS WHO LOSE CUSTODY

Mothers Without Custody is a national self-help organization for noncustodial mothers living apart from their children. Their purpose is to enhance quality of life for children by strengthening the role of the non-custodial parent through sharing information and experiences. There is a newsletter and chapters nation-wide.

For more information send a long, self-addressed stamped envelope to:

Mothers Without Custody (MWOC)
Box 56762
Houston, TX 77256-6762
(713)840-1622

or read:

MOTHERS WITHOUT CUSTODY
by Jeffrey Grief and Mary Pabst
(Lexington Books, 1988)

ABSENTEE MOTHERS
by Patricia Packowicz
(Universe Books, 1982)

Women bear the burden as well as the gift of motherhood. The assumption that nurturing is gene-related is unfair to women as well as men. Studies indicate that at least a third of the mothers who give up their children do not feel guilty because they believe it was for the benefit of their children. Others regret their decision years later. Primary care of children is not necessarily for everyone, but being a parent is each parent's responsibility. How that is executed can take many forms.

My parents divorced when I was four, and at age eight I was given my choice of who to live with. Neither was financially well-off. I chose my father because we got along better. I love both my parents. Custody didn't matter to me because I could see both of them. And I still do.
—Adult female caller ("Phil Donahue Show"
dealing with noncustodial mothers)

KEEPING YOUR EX-SPOUSE FROM BEING AN EX-PARENT

Unfortunately, sole custody means, by definition, that one parent has lost custody. Being an unempowered parent becomes painful, and absence often becomes easier than dealing with the visitation schedule of legal access to your children. Yes, there are parents who don't care to give or nurture, but often it is the loss of normal accessibility to their children that makes absentee parents.

The custodial parent may suffer from the seemingly unending responsibility for the children, whereas the noncustodial parent suffers from feeling cut out of the children's lives. The custodial parent has the undeniable advantage of being the decision maker, whereas the noncustodial parent has the advantage of more free time. Each is jealous of the other's advantages and much less aware of his own. If there's a great deal of anger, distrust, and disapproval between the parents, it may be difficult for the one with custody to encourage involvement of the other. But children do have a right to know and love both parents, and in all but the most unusual of circumstances, the noncustodial parent has a right to see and spend time with the kids. Even when a legal custody agreement mandates a certain amount of visiting time, the noncustodial parent too often becomes discouraged because of the discomfort of "visiting" time, and having to deal with the other parent and their own lack of control. They often gradually fade out of their children's lives.

Men whose wives initiate divorce proceedings often stop seeing their children. This may occur for just a few months or it may continue over the years. Sometimes this withdrawal is out of anger at the wife or just results from hurt and grief. A man in this situation can reason that if he is unwanted by his wife, he is unwanted or unneeded by his children.

The primary caretaker parent can help make contact easier and encourage regular contact with the children, even though it takes extra effort if a lot of anger is still present. It is a time when you must separate your spousal relationship from your parenting relationship. This is hard, but it *IS* possible. You must try not to "direct" your spouse's parenting patterns and concentrate your efforts on smoothing access.

Men who have been competent, involved fathers B.D. (Before Divorce) can and should continue their fathering afterward. One study indicates that fathers who stay connected during the first year of a divorce stay involved. Some women are often glad when their children don't see too much of Dad, because they don't want him to be a significant role model. But lack of contact and familiarity with the other parent is not

*My children lived with their mother, 300 miles away.
Every trip to see them was difficult because of the drive,
anxiety about how the kids would be, and the difficulties
with my ex-wife. The kids and I would go to a motel, get
reacquainted, and in the two days I'd feel like a father
again. The trip home was always awful, and I'd have to
readjust to the loss of them again. I finally decided it
would be easier for all to stop the trips. I always sent my
support check and I never missed a birthday or Christmas. As I didn't know what to buy them, I'd just send
checks. When the kids were grown, each came to me
separately and let me know how much they resented my
disappearance from their lives. Each let me know that
they would have preferred the pain of the visits to my
having become just a "check" in their lives.*

—Unsigned, noncustodial father

a guarantee that your child will be free of bad habits or
poor traits exemplified by your ex.

A family today is defined more by its common history than by its blood tie. Deny a parent sharing in that
history of your children's growing up and he or she
won't feel—or act—much like a parent.

IT DOESN'T MATTER HOW YOU FEEL ABOUT THE OTHER PARENT; IT ONLY MATTERS HOW YOU ACT.

Encouraging Good Access (Visitation) Time

Some of the following suggestions can help you
separate your feelings from your deeds. If you are the
custodial parent, you will set the tone for visitation
and thus how well it can work for your child. If you
want your ex to respect and listen to your parenting

parameters, then it's necessary that you do the same.
Being flexible yourself, first, will usually be the key to
your ex's flexibility. Try to:

• Imagine yourself as the "visiting" parent. Would
  you like the schedule?
• Keep access schedules as regular as possible, and
  don't cancel a child's visit with the other parent
  unless it's absolutely necessary.
• Plan holiday and vacation visits far enough ahead
  so that children old enough to have a concept of
  time will know what's going to happen.
• Discuss specific child-rearing problems you're having. Often the other parent is having the same problem and a joint strategy can produce better behavior
  and improved time together for each parent.
• Don't interfere with the other parent's style of parenting. Do not tell your child that the other parent
  shouldn't let him or her stay up late. Just set your
  bedtime rules and stick to them.
• Encourage frequent communication between the kids
  and the other parent through telephone calls and
  notes. Don't use calls from the other parent to the
  children as opportunities for arguments or to discuss money, or he or she will stop calling.
• Let the other parent know how much you appreciate his or her behavior and scheduled time with the
  children (even if you must search the depths of
  your being to find the kind words). Tell your ex
  that you want him or her to be an important part of
  your children's lives.
• Help maintain the good working relationship you
  need with the other parent by occasional phone
  calls to share some of the good things that happen
  to the kids when they're with you—a new skill
  learned, a good report card—and not just the problems.

Now that he was officially, legally, the visiting (or visited)
father, something remarkable happened. At thirty-five
years of age, he chose paternity. This time he really
chose it. Out of loneliness and guilt at first, and out of
pleasure at last, the visited father finally established a
rapport with his children. He spent more time with them
in ten months than he had in ten years. Alone with his
children, he took intensive on-the-job training. He be-
came the kind of parent who knew how to braid hair and
limit junk food and tuck in tired bodies—and yell. Alone
with his children, he found them to be remarkably inter-
esting. The visiting father who never had time for his
children made time.
　　　　—Ellen Goodman, The Boston Globe, June 14, 1977

Women are often more flexible in accepting a variety of standards in day care for their children than
they are in accepting anything less than the way they
themselves would parent from an ex-husband. Children can be cared for by less than "adequate" noncustodial fathers and flourish because the father cares
about the kids. Caring counts for more than the me-
chanics of the job.

Encourage your ex-spouse to go with you to school
conferences. Your mutual reluctance to be together
will be offset by the children's pleasure in finding that
their school lives are of primary importance to both
parents. Hearing nice things about our children together reaffirms the good that your marriage produced.
Try to alternate conferences if you can't do it together.
If there are school problems to be dealt with, parent-
teacher conferences can be constructive events to work
out a shared plan of parenting tactics.

On a Practical Level

- Get into the habit of making extra copies of photos of the kids so they can share them with their other parent and relatives.
- Remind your child to invite his or her other parent to important events or performances.
- Send along some schoolwork with the child to the other parent on a regular basis.
- Don't schedule after-school or weekend activities for a child without first discussing it with the parent whose time will be affected.
- Encourage kids' participation, from keeping notes on daily doings (maybe a diary) so they can share specifics when the other parent asks what they're doing to maintaining their own calendars to keep track of when they'll be visiting the noncustodial parent.
- Allow favorite toys and books to travel with your child, even if they are special gifts from you.
- Take the trouble to help the children select cards and gifts for the other parent's birthday and for holidays. (Gifts from you are your own decision.)

A friend divorced when her son was four years old, and her ex-husband moved 1,000 miles away. Every summer she put her son on a plane for a month's visitation. He came home with tales that indicated his father's lack of interest in him, yet he continued to want to visit. Some years she would wonder, "Why am I permitting this charade?" especially the summer he hired a baby-sitter for one of the four weeks his son was with him, and went camping with friends. However, she was rewarded for those years of encouraging visitation, when her son came home at age fourteen and said, "Mom, this summer while I was with Dad, I could finally understand why you divorced him."

—Unsigned

- Provide a list of the children's regular baby-sitters so your children won't have to adjust to a new one. (Yes, you must accept that your ex will not spend every waking moment with his or her child, even during limited times together.)
- Ease pickups and drop-offs using the suggestions given on page 181.

The Unreliable Parent

Many noncustodial parents are not punctual or are otherwise unreliable about visitation. There are many possible reasons for this. Some parents are just not responsible or punctual for anything. Divorce doesn't change or improve that. Some are truly not interested in their children, but many others are uncomfortable about their new role with the children, afraid of their children's feelings, unsure how to behave with them, and so on.

Most children, especially younger children, would prefer some visitation, however unreliable, to none. It is often hard for the custodial parent to accept this preference. There is very little you can do to help, except let your children talk about their feelings. If you, as an adult, are being inconvenienced by waiting for hours, you can tell your ex that you will wait 45 minutes and then leave with the children. You may have to do that a few times to get the point across. In the long run your children will be better off if you handle it in a matter-of-fact manner. Unreliability may bother you more than it does the children. After all, they probably understand that parent's weaknesses.

My dad never showed up when he said he would. Many a day I spent sitting in the window, my bag packed, waiting and watching for him, and he never came. When I look back on it, I wonder how my mom stood it. Yet she never said anything. She let me wait and watch while she went on about her business. It was so much better for me that she let me do what I needed to do.

—Unsigned

MAKING IT EASIER ON THE KIDS

Troubling as visits are for adults, they're also tough on kids. If you can manage it, there are ways to help them:

- Speak positively to the kids about their other parent. If it's not possible to hide your anger, at least express it in ways that make clear that the problems are between you and your ex-spouse—do not involve the children. (For example, "I guess your father and I don't see eye to eye on that issue.")
- Be civil to your ex-spouse when you happen to be together; open hostility hurts and tears at the children's loyalty bonds.
- Don't force the children to become involved in adult business by having them convey your messages (pickup times, money due, and such) to the other parent. Use the phone and the mail for your own communication.
- Don't pump your child for personal information about the other parent.
- Be gracious about letting the children talk about and show enthusiasm for the other parent's living

quarters and for the things they do with him or her, even if you have to bite your tongue.

- Don't try to mediate conflicts or involve yourself in arguments between your child and your ex. Remember that although you can help, the noncustodial parent is ultimately responsible for maintaining a personal relationship with the kids.
- Encourage your children not to *blame* the parent who initiated the divorce. Help them see how anger (yes, even justified anger) really only hurts us—never the person we are angry at.

Don't belittle your former spouse to a child. An adolescent will despise you for it, and a younger child will be confused and unhappy. Remember, even if you and your new partner have custody and are paying all the bills, the parent who only visits has some stake in the child, too.
— Unsigned, divorced mother

I still remember as a child standing in the driveway crying, waiting for my dad to pick us up. There were many times he didn't come. Years later I learned that when my parents would fight, she would tell him not to come see us. She didn't tell us he wasn't coming so he would look bad in our eyes.
— Charmaine Rusu, Phoenix, AZ

Small children, in particular, often keep the absent parent on a pedestal. Such hero-worship will tax your tolerance. Don't let resentment make you say things you don't really mean (or may *really* mean) to your child. Remember, you're the grown-up. No one said it would be easy. It's hard to keep a rational perspective when your child returns from time spent with the other parent with a glowing report. A special outing or a small toy seems to outweigh the value of all your custodial chores of the week.

Does this fit your situation? Just stop and remember to be thankful that the other parent cares and has stayed involved with the children. Being cared about and catered to is what kids need. Don't stand in judgment of the inappropriateness of your ex's attention. The kids aren't criticizing *YOU* when they express pleasure in a visit with your ex. If necessary, work on some self-talk, reminding yourself of all the positive, caring, unselfish things you do for your kids. Your kids aren't going to stroke you; neither is your ex. It's okay to do this for yourself!

When a now-distanced parent stops coming around, a child is not going to blame you or the other parent. A child will place the blame on him or herself. A child will feel, "I must have done something wrong or been bad because Daddy (Mommy) doesn't want to see me anymore." It may help for you to explain to a child how painful "visiting" is for a noncustodial parent so the child's self-blame is lessened. Of course, this is not an easy task for a custodial parent; it's simply a necessary one! If your former spouse is not spending time with the children, ask for an explanation. Then share that explanation with your children. They must understand that they are not the cause of the lack of visitation. Remember:

PARENTS, NO MATTER WHAT
THEIR ARRANGEMENTS ARE,
DON'T LOSE THEIR LOVE FOR
THEIR CHILDREN. THEY MAY,
HOWEVER, LOSE THEIR ABILITY
TO SHOW IT.

"Reentry" and "Off-the-Wall"

Visitation parenting is new for the now-distant parent, but it is also new to a child. Children often seem troublesome, overactive, and uncooperative on returning home after a visit with the noncustodial parent. The common expression is that they are "bouncing off the walls." This problematic transitional situation may take six months to a year to stabilize, but it will. In the meantime, help by keeping consistent routines, and don't be tempted to consider this as a reason for your child not to see the other parent.

You can ease this transition by:

- Your own awareness and expectation of this syndrome. This will be your most effective tool for dealing with it. When you expect the behavior, you can prepare yourself for it.
- Let it be "safe" for your kids to express conflicting feelings once back on home turf. Returning reminds them that they can't have both parents together, so they are both happy and unhappy at returning home and leaving the noncustodial parent.
- Watching a favorite TV show or video can get kids back into the rhythm of your household. You can also involve them in playing a game, listening to music, cooking something, or doing a puzzle.
- Eating a meal or snack helps kids settle into your routine.
- Think of your child's reaction as being much like how you feel when you arrive home from a vacation: You probably don't want to unpack and you're not quite sure how to settle in.

Be tolerant of the clinging, crying child who doesn't want the noncustodial parent to leave. It's a natural reaction that will ease with time. It might also be a sign that the child needs more time with that other parent. It isn't a bad reflection on you. And for the child who returns in a disheveled state (cranky or dirty or exhausted), yes, reentry will be harder on you and your child. But two different homes can have different rules. If the kids' time spent with the noncustodial parent was good for them, avoid criticism and stretch your tolerance levels.

KEEPING YOURSELF (THE NONCUSTODIAL PARENT) FROM BEING AN EX-PARENT

Many assume the single parent without custody has the easiest time adjusting. But a noncustodial parent deals with a paradox. Although glad to be away from the scene of a bad marriage and perhaps feeling relief at being free of the daily responsibility of children, he or she often has to fight loneliness, guilt, and depression. There's often anger at being denied the chance of making parental decisions, at losing the intimacy that parenting brings, and the accompanying feelings of powerlessness.

Most noncustodial parents are fathers, and they often are unaccustomed to caring for the children's needs and unfamiliar with child-care routines—just as some women are unfamiliar with managing their finances. But as fathers, they can and will learn, given the chance. Their styles may differ from Mom's but that doesn't mean they can't perform satisfactorily. And, Dad, never hide behind the rationalization that because you never did much for them before, the kids won't miss you now. They will. Fathers need to figure out how to father without living in the same household. As a visiting parent, it is easy to become an outsider in the lives of your children. Fathering from afar is not only possible, but rewarding. It will take time and practice. Be patient . . . with yourself and your former spouse.

How do you keep yourself from becoming an ex-parent if you are the noncustodial parent who must live within the limitation of access constraints? The answer:

CONSISTENCY . . . FREQUENCY . . . PREDICTABILITY

Let your children know they can count on you. Infrequent contact tells them—by your actions—that they can't. Live up to your commitments, both financial and otherwise. Missed support payments can result in more anger and alienation that the children ultimately hear about. Frequent canceling or postponing of visits gives kids the message that you don't care about them or consider them important. Beyond that:

- Make your home your children's home, too, by keeping familiar pictures and other items around and by displaying their artwork. Be sure there's a place for each one's belongings, if only a drawer or closet shelf. Introduce them to the new neighborhood by taking walks and watching for other kids of the same ages.
- Keep special articles like swimsuits or boots at your home. You can easily duplicate these rarely used items by picking them up at secondhand stores, being open to receiving hand-me-downs, or buying them on sale.
- Encourage the kids to bring homework along and keep arts and crafts' supplies on hand so they can work or play alone sometimes. You'll find there's less pressure on all of you if you don't spend every minute of a visit doing something special together.

Part-time parents often try to pack everything into each visit. Don't. Relax. In time, you and your children will become comfortable with your new living arrangements.

- Let each child bring a guest occasionally. Keep in mind, however, that it's easier on the kids if you don't have your social partners over at their first visits, or later, at every visit.

- Try to have some private time with each child when they visit together, and periodically have each one visit separately. One-on-one time is important and memorable quality time. Most custodial spouses would be comfortable with extra time taken with a child alone even if it means they don't get their own "time off" on occasion.

- Make your mid-week visit a time when you take your child to an activity or lesson. It will be a helpful, relaxed, and normal use of time with your child where you don't have to feel the need to entertain.

- Keep in touch with the kids' school and outside activities. If you live in the same town, try to attend events your children participate in. Let school personnel know that you expect to be informed about progress or problems, and make every effort to attend conferences and school events. (Unfortunately if the other parent is the sole custodian, legally the school doesn't have to keep you informed other than about grades.)

- Make report-card time an event, such as "dinner out." It will help insure that your child will let you know when it arrives.

- Decide that you will not play a minor role in your children's lives. Telephone daily, go to some classes together, develop a common interest that is easy to share on visits as well as when you are apart, such as maintaining a tropical fish collection.

- Be aware of a child's frustrations that may be vented in words such as "I want to go back to Mommy's." Encourage use of the phone at such times, and try to be tolerant.

Never let a custodial parent's negative attitude or barriers ever get in the way of letting your child know just how much you care for that child.

Outing Ideas for Weekend Parents

It's a hard balance—not wanting to compete with the custodial spouse, yet wanting to show your kids a good time. Under normal family circumstances, one parent NEVER spends long one-on-one time like this with his or her kids. Noncustodial fathers often find themselves in the position of now having a 7- or 12-year-old as a constant weekend companion, which wouldn't be the case if the family was together. It's realistic that the noncustodial parent resents the emotional (and often financial) drain of these concentrated times together. Be patient. With time, entertainment and outings shift to more natural quality time together. Remember, what children need is a parent, not an entertainer or "camp director." Don't overcompensate. Let them have a say about where you'll go and what you'll do, but spend some quiet time at home, too. Assign chores and set disciplinary guidelines similar to those they're used to. Remember, too, that:

- Successful outings take preplanning. Be it assembling paraphernalia or just allocating time, think ahead.
- A child-oriented guidebook to your city can give a complete listing of new ideas.
- Airports, duck ponds, and shopping malls are fine settings for outings.

- Libraries often offer free reading and movie hours.
- If you live near bus or train transportation, a day trip to a location an hour or two away makes a long day more manageable.
- A country outing, such as camping or picking corn or berries or just visiting a nearby farm, is usually enjoyed by children who range widely in age.
- A visit to a beach for sand play keeps kids happy for hours. You can also share in the building of a sand castle.
- Starting a hobby or collection together offers great opportunities for one-on-one time. Rocks are usually inexpensive to collect; model building is a good continuing project, as is putting together a jigsaw puzzle.

Concentrate on activities that build relationships, not those that distract you from getting to know one another. Remind yourself that children have their own cycles, phases, and stages . . . just as they did when you all lived together! Do your homework. Read up on child development and pick up some parenting books to expand your caring and coping skills.

THE LONG-DISTANCE, OUT-OF-STATE PARENT

Distance has nothing to do with letting a child feel loved and missed. It may always be a painful barrier for a long-distance parent, but sincerity, consistency, and extra verbal assurances can make up for a lot of miles. Other than holiday or summer visitation, the two primary ways a long-distance noncustodial parent communicates are by mail and by phone. Sometimes, an aggressive and energetic long-distance parent's communication may create feelings of anger, anxiety, and jealousy with a hostile custodial parent. These feelings, although understandable, are truly misplaced and only make it harder on the children. In a long-distance situation there is really no other place but the custodial parent's "turf" for the distanced parent-child relationship to exist for the major part of the year.

I had six years of joint custodial parenting before my kids moved when their mother remarried. It hurts having them gone. The telephone is a big help. We talk several times a week. They call me for advice. Accepting that they are better off where they are helps, but I still miss them.
—Howard Rutman, Minneapolis, MN

When one parent moves to deny their children a relationship with the other parent and discourages their communication, it always backfires in time. Acting-out behavior on the part of children surfaces, or children's anger will be directed at the custodial parent. Yes, your children will eventually blame you, the custodial parent. The key word here is *courtesy* on the part of both parents. Discretion and self-control are valuable in keeping long-distance channels open. There will probably be the occasional slip, when inappropriate words are said. Forgive yourself and/or your ex and keep going. Don't let a momentary flare-up get in the way of keeping up the faraway parent's connection with his or her kids.

The courts have never honestly addressed the financial burdens of parenting long-distance. They tend to be ignored or underestimated. Try to accept that all these costs are simply *extra* and think of them as you would any other investment with long-term benefits. Sadly, the distant father who can't measure up financially and afford these extra costs will also bear the additional social stigma for not "making enough." It is an unfortunate situation.

Keeping the Lines Open from a Distance

Custodial and noncustodial parents can do a number of things to make long-distance parenting easier:

- Always begin a call by asking if this is a good time to talk. If you've hit meal time, kids are put in the middle and must try to accommodate both parents. The cost of calling back is small compared to creating mixed feelings.
- Don't put the custodial parent in the position of having to pay for long-distance phone calls. Children should be taught how to reverse the charges or be given an access number to a long-distance phone service.
- When calling on holidays or special occasions, consider the custodial parent's schedule. Predetermined times for phone calls are usually helpful.
- Weekends are convenient for phone calls; rates are lowest and timing is more flexible.
- If your budget allows, try watching a TV show or TV sports event "together" by phone for a while, long-distance.
- If your budget is tight, send taped messages back and forth.
- Keep a running list (like a grocery list) of things you'd like to discuss or share with the kids during the week. Encourage your children to do the same.
- Thank the custodial parent for keeping the lines of communication open and pass on any other "warm fuzzies" you can bring yourself to give. It's good business management.

- As the custodial parent, try to give helpful options without sounding like you are controlling access time. An unempowered parent already is at a disadvantage. Let him or her have some "win" situations.

The Written Connection

Children love to receive mail, so write as often as you can. When writing, use appropriate style, vocabulary, and handwriting (or typing) for your child's age and ability. The more creative and exciting the letter, the better chance it will have of being read.

This is not the time to preach and teach. The absent parent often has a strong urge to err in this direction to prove his or her parenting effectiveness. And if you are going to make written comments about your ex, be sure they are positive. (Trust me, this will also work to your advantage.) You should assume that all correspondence will be read by the custodial parent mainly because your child will want to share his or her good news. Also:

- For children 4–6 years of age, include pictures cut from magazines and photos. Most kids also love riddles.
- Try coded messages for elementary-school children. These can be sent in postcard form after the initial code "dictionary" is sent. (Receiving a new postcard each day can be great fun for children who love mail.)
- For readers, clip and send articles that you can discuss. Obviously, favorite topics should be picked —computers, new fashion trends, whatever your child is interested in. Antidrug and antirock music messages will probably not be well received.
- Send a cute contemporary card when you don't have much to say.

- Work up a game of chess or checkers you can play by mail.
- Provide your children with a stack of self-addressed, stamped envelopes or postcards. (You might include some addressed to the grandparents, too.)

If your ex has remarried, include the new spouse in the correspondence. Children should be encouraged to maintain good relationships with stepparents; they are additions to their lives, not replacements of you.

FIRST AID FOR KEEPING CONNECTED

101 WAYS TO BE A LONG DISTANCE SUPER-DAD by George Neuman, 1983 (Blossom Valley Press, Mountain View, CA 94040), gives lots of helpful tips and ideas in a concise paperback book.

LONG DISTANCE PARENTING by Miriam Galper Cohen (NAL, 1989). A guidebook specifically focused on keeping the long-distance connections intact and growing.

THE WRITTEN CONNECTION, a package of materials for a noncustodial parent. It contains twelve months of structured communication materials, providing for four mailings per month, plus a guidebook. For kids aged 3–10. (Indicate your child's age.) Send $49.95 plus $5 postage to:
The Written Connection
PO Box 572
Chandler, AZ 85224
or call 1-800-334-3143 (AZ 602-926-7287)

(A three-month starter kit is available for $9.95.)

Summertime Parent

Some divorced parents share legal custody of the children but are forced by circumstances to have physical custody only during vacations. Others are noncustodial parents whose visitation arrangements include these lengthy periods. Both may have difficulties getting reacquainted with the kids after long separations. And both are likely to find caring for them and keeping them entertained for a long period stressful as well as delightful. To help yourself and your kids:

- If you haven't seen them for several months or a year, be prepared for great changes in the kids. Children grow and become different little people, it seems, and all children develop new habits, and likes and dislikes.
- Don't look on the visit as one long period of fun and games. It's important for both you and the kids to have a normal kind of life that includes both work and play and to have time alone as well as with each other.
- Don't cut out all your own social activities for the duration of the kids' visit. They need to see you have an interesting life that continues when they are not with you, so that they don't experience feelings of guilt and pity about your loneliness.
- Take advantage of whatever your community offers in the way of appropriate children's activities: library story hours, park programs, religious or other day camps. Encourage the kids to make friends and see other children.

Check the ideas on pages 159–160; they are also applicable here.

Children have to deal with their leave-taking at the end of the visit. Good-byes are seldom easy on anyone. There may be anger. There may be sadness. Reduce anxiety by being specific about when you'll talk and visit next.

7

Joint Custody: A Sharing Parenting Option

My bias is toward joint physical and legal custody because, with continuing adjustments, it has worked for me and my children (and, I think, for my ex-husband, too). No, this arrangement doesn't take the place of my fantasy of the perfect family life—it's different, but it's been workable. Shared parenting was obvious to me before I even understood the term. I knew I didn't want to be denied access to my children more than half of the time, so I could never consider anything less for my ex. Many other parents who work at shared physical custody apparently agree with me. In a study of metropolitan New York parents after a year of shared custody, 80 percent said they would recommend it, even though only 7 percent reported no problems with the arrangement.

Probably most important to the success of any shared parenting is seeing it work for your children. My ex-husband and I were aided by the facts that we lived 2 miles apart, that the children stayed in the same school system, and that neither of us had plans to remarry or even had an obvious "significant other." We started out sharing the week, but after a few months we found that it was difficult for the kids (then ages 10 and 13) to move twice a week, so we switched to a weekly arrangement. After a while we became so flexible that sometimes "moving time" was decided less than 24 hours in advance. It worked although we had little personal or phone contact. As adults, we tried to accommodate each other's schedules when possible and asked that the children always call the other house before dropping in unexpectedly. Among the never-ending annoyances were the extra trips someone had to make when schoolbooks or sporting gear were left in the wrong house. I've found that these instances became problems only if we let them. (And on long, stressful days, sometimes I did.) Things changed once our son turned 16 and could drive back and forth himself. In fact, given our flexible schedule we had to make sure the other parent knew when he was changing residences so he didn't "fall through the crack" of a weekend with both of us thinking he was with the other parent.

Actually I kind of like the two homes. When I seem to have worn out my welcome at one place, it's time to change and I start out fresh with the other parent.
—Douglas Lansky, age 15

POSITIVE ASPECTS OF JOINT CUSTODY

Children of joint custody benefit by having more time with each parent, and the extra parenting time on and off benefits the parents. Joint custody also has time advantages for the careers of parents. Some families have based their joint custody at Dad's house while Mom completes her education. Or Mom can afford to take a job requiring travel, knowing the children will be well cared for. The benefits of personal time off are significant, too. You have time for per-

sonal growth and self-definition that helps you learn
about yourself outside of your parenting role.

Child-support payments often increase under joint
custody, because fathers who do not feel unfairly de-
prived of their parental rights are more likely to fulfill
their financial obligations. One study found that 56
percent of mothers with sole custody returned to court
because their former spouses refused to pay child support, whereas none of the mothers having joint custody
returned to court over money issues. Although conflict
is difficult to measure, statistics show that only half of
parents with joint custody relitigate their disputes as
compared to those with sole custody arrangements. As
someone said, "It stands to reason that when parents
are around, their wallets are around."

Data indicate that joint custody works best financially for higher-income and lower-income families.
Lower-income families share their scarce economic
resources as well as their time resources. One study
of Aid For Dependent Children fathers showed that,
on average, they have more contact with their children
than non-AFDC fathers. Lower-income families' (usually de facto) joint custody allows for new job training,
different work shifts, and shared child care.

Some experts even feel that joint custody can increase the likelihood of having cooperative parenting
after divorce. Living cooperatively as husband and
wife is different than cooperative parenting. Inability
to handle the former does not rule out success for the
latter. Don't hide behind the idea that if you could
work out something this complex in your marriage,
you wouldn't be divorcing now. It's not true. Joint
custody is easier if everyone is accommodating, but it
is not necessary. A 1984 study at the University of
Delaware found that parents with joint custody arrangements, get along no better or worse with their

ex-spouses than those in sole custody situations. Recent research indicated that despite parental animosity, shared parenting is not only possible—it works!

Legal Leanings

Joint custody empowers women by having fathers share in child rearing. In 1980 only three states accepted joint custody. Now it's the presumption or preference in more than 13 of the 41 states that now accept it. Judges, for the most part, have been convinced of the viability of joint custody. In a landmark decision, the New Jersey Supreme Court, in endorsing physical and legal joint custody, set the following guidelines:

- Joint custody may be ordered over the objection of a parent.
- An amicable relationship between parents is not a prerequisite to an award of joint custody.
- The assessment for cooperation should not be made in the emotional heat of a divorce.
- A parent who refuses to cooperate with a joint custody order may forfeit custody altogether.

In establishing these guidelines, the court's basic requirement was whether the child had established a sufficient relationship with both parents, not whether the parents had been equally involved in the child rearing. Courts in some states have even given joint custody in contested cases against the wishes of a parent.

I enjoy life with my Dad and I like my life with my Mom. Actually, switching homes has been a good experience for me.

—Shira Rutman, age 11

Obviously, joint custody will work differently for
each family, but it works best when:

- Both parents are interested in shared parenting.
- Parents' income resources are high enough to support two complete homes.
- Both parents are physically and emotionally able to
  act as parents, and both parents' jobs are flexible
  enough so they can be available for emergencies.
- Parents can separate their personal conflicts from
  their parenting roles, communicate reasonably well,
  and cooperate with each other on matters that affect
  the children.
- Parents have similar styles and agree on basic values and on some common house rules. Each parent
  can respect—or at least accept—each other's values
  and parenting styles.
- Parents live close enough to each other and can
  alternate days or weeks with school children.

It also helps when children are old enough to handle
the frequent moving between the two homes. A study
by Wallerstein and McKennon indicates that young
preschool children may not adapt to shifting homes as
well as older preschoolers. Young preschoolers usually need more consistency in their lives than equally
shared physical custody offers. Still, you will have to
evaluate your child honestly and decide whether he or
she is better off sleeping at the home of one parent
every night and seeing the other on the custodial parent's turf (perhaps even every day), or making frequent
moves. As they get older, children can eventually spend
weekends with the other parent, then gradually stay
for longer periods. By elementary years, alternating
weeks with each parent is often workable, whereas
two-week stays at one address may be too long. Teens
will let you know their comfort level for moving. All

kids seem to indicate that although going back and forth is not easy, it is preferable to not having significant time with the other parent.

In joint custody, it is common and perhaps even best for kids to have an "anchor" home (one where most of their possessions remain, where the school sends report cards, and where they pack for summer camp). Yet many children seem to be able to adjust to the reality of two different—or even equal—places they can call home.

"If someone asked you, 'Where do you live, Jamie?' what would you say?"
"I live at my mom's and my dad's," explained Jamie.
"It's complicated but it's not confusing to me."
                          —from Sharing Parenthood After Divorce,
                          Ciji Ware (Viking, 1982)

Geography obviously becomes an important custody issue when shared parenting is a life-style. Many parents have chosen child-care considerations over career considerations in shared parenting situations. Others have stretched their imaginations and resources to accommodate long-distance shared parenting. It's not easy, but it is possible. Still others find children coming to live with them as they grow older and their needs change.

"Power struggles in parenting, not two households, whether in joint or sole custody situations, are what usually cause confusion for kids," believes Gary Kretchmer, who works the Tenth Judicial District of Kansas. "When the noncustodial parent is granted joint custody, the fight is usually over and the situation calms down. I strongly believe that joint custody reduces hassles and conflict. Joint custody says nothing about two parents agreeing, only that issues will be discussed. Having one's views being recognized can go a long way toward solving problems."

Why Some Think Joint Custody Can Be Less than Desirable

Although a good solution for many families, joint custody does have its problems—it's not a perfect solution. Some believe that it has been a King Solomon-type solution, where the child is emotionally cut in half. Children not only have to contend with Mom's house rules and Dad's, but perhaps Mom's church and Dad's church, Mom's friends and Dad's friends as well. (Yet children learn to cope with different rules in other domains, such as school or camp or scouts.) Some claim that the need for contact through shared parenting keeps a couple tied together and thus allows a child's hopes for reconciliation to continue. But couples who have experienced joint custody can attest to the fallacy of this argument. To those who have argued that it is bad for children to have two homes, the universal reply has been, "It's better to have two parents."

Research from the Center for the Family in Transition indicates that for the 5 percent of truly bitter contested divorces they studied, children do fare worse in frequent visitation situations that are often categorized as joint custody. Jan Johnston, Director of Research for the Center, cautions against today's pressure to have only joint custody, when, like everything else, no one parenting option will be appropriate for every family.

For some children joint custody can be confusing; for others it's a chance to see two different life-style options. Do children suffer from emotional "jet lag" when they switch homes? Probably some do. If joint custody is too stressful for your child, then it's not appropriate for your family. Then, too, some parents feel that joint custody can cripple the parenting ability of one of the parents. This may depend on each person's need to be in charge or the belief that we actually can control such matters. It's difficult to be fair about the double chores that kids can be faced with, such as mowing two lawns, folding family laundry twice a week, and such. (And the Sock Dragon, who hides in the laundry room, makes out doubly well in joint physical custodial arrangements.)

Hardest for children to deal with is the pull that two homes create. Packing, unpacking, and planning take away from essential "downtime" and the need to sometimes just stop and be "home" without switching homes. For many kids, trying to accommodate two parents' lives, two parents' homes, takes time and energy. We parents don't have to pack up and move every week or month or summer. There is no simple solution here but being sensitive to the tired traveler and being flexible enough to change schedules without feeling threatened by such changes (short- or long-term) can help take the pressure off a child.

Another aspect of the dilemma of joint physical custody is pointed out by Phyllis Chesler in her book *Mothers On Trial* (McGraw-Hill, 1986). She believes that mothers become impoverished as they make financial settlements to their disadvantage in joint custody arrangements out of fear of losing custody or facing a custody battle.

Still, the emotional boost for fathers must not be discounted. Fathers who are forced (or feel pressured) to give up their children become depressed, can't sleep, or concentrate on their jobs, and may even contemplate suicide. Even fathers with joint custodial visitation schedules have better and longer-term involvement with their children and greater personal self-esteem than do noncustodial fathers. Finally, the threat of single fathers being cut off from their children is fading as courts lean toward joint legal custody even when the mother maintains physical custody.

One consideration we have in our neighborhood where several families have joint physical custody arrangements is that when my children are with me, their neighborhood friends are often off with their other parent and not around for my kids to play with. I often find myself checking out my neighbor's custodial arrangements when I'm planning our schedules.

—Suzanne Lang, Minnetonka, MN

SETTING UP THE GROUND RULES FOR SHARING PHYSICAL CUSTODY

Putting as much in writing as possible for a shared parenting situation is a good idea, if only to help you work through the details and anticipate the "what ifs." In some states, a judge must see and approve a written agreement and will have the right to ask questions and require certain changes. Children old enough to understand the agreement may be allowed to read it or have it read to them. The circumstances special to each family will dictate the terms of the contract, but some issues are universal. And almost no detail is too minor to consider if there is any possibility there may be misunderstandings.

In the beginning there is frequent communication and confusion, but with time any system can work smoothly and require little contact between the parents. To help in making joint custody smoother:

- Talk about the children's religious education and who will take care of the transportation.
- Come to reasonable agreements about house rules and general living patterns that are of special concern to either parent. A difference of a few minutes in bedtime or the requirement to do more chores at one house may not be terribly important; kids usually adjust easily to different sets of rules, as long as they are consistent in each home. On the other hand, television limitations or getting a child's hair cut by the same barber every time may matter very much to one parent or the other.
- Plan to set up master calendars at each home and to meet or talk on the phone often enough to keep them up to date and accurate. Or let the more detail-oriented parent make up a monthly master calendar and photocopy it for the other.
- Be specific about issues of responsibility and payment for expenses that fall outside the norm of child support. Child support might cover dental bills, but will it also cover braces? Will it cover a teen's car payments or car insurance?
- Make decisions ahead of time about handling school problems and attending conferences and school events. For example, should an opposite-gender friend of one parent be invited to school activities?
- Avoid last-minute surprises. Sudden changes in plans cause anger, disappointment, and loss of trust.
- Agree that all decisions concerning division of responsibilities and time spent with each parent will be reevaluated periodically and that adjustments will be negotiated when necessary. Keep in mind that as children grow, schedules change.

Children may become expert packers but they still get tired of it. Be tolerant of forgotten items. Moving back and forth creates the need for items you dupli-

Despite the fact that we had appropriate tote bags, the
kids seemed to always be transporting their belongings
in brown paper grocery bags. After a certain age it didn't
matter if you had two of things—they had their favorite
jeans, shirts, etc. that had to go back and forth. Nor did
they want to unpack right away when they arrived. That
was too hard on me. I'd unpack their "bags." It actually
made their "reentry" easier on me.

—Elaine Tharler, Wellesley, MA

cate (toothpaste), items you divide (toys or stuffed
animals), and items that simply go back and forth
(sports uniforms).

TO HELP PLAN OUT YOUR CO-PARENTING SCHEDULES

If you are planning on a joint physical custody situation, these three books, each with different viewpoints,
are excellent guides.

*MOM'S HOUSE, DAD'S HOUSE:
Making Shared Custody Work
by Isolina Ricci
(Macmillan, 1980)

SHARED PARENTHOOD AFTER DIVORCE
by Ciji Ware
(Viking/Bantam, 1982)

JOINT CUSTODY AND CO-PARENTING:
Sharing Your Child Equally
by Miriam Galper
(Running Press, revised 1980)

*See page 244.

Another resource for information is the Joint Custody Association, 10606 Wilkins Ave., Los Angeles, CA 90024 (213)475-5352. This association, headed by James Cooke, author of the California Joint Custody legislation, will answer any of your questions as well as send out informational material.

Handling the Glitches

Making arrangements and adhering to them are two different matters. Nothing runs perfectly all the time. And very little runs perfectly in the beginning. When you remember your own childhood or the days when your marriage was working well and your family was intact, you're likely to think only about the good times, glossing over the problems. The glitches in shared parenting may not be exactly the same as those of earlier days, but they can almost always be solved in the same ways—by facing them squarely and by trying to view them as challenges to your ingenuity and intelligence instead of as unsolvable disasters. This involves:

- Knowing that some youngsters feel that parents often take the logistical complications more seriously than the kids—and they're right. When in doubt, see a situation through your child's eyes.
- Remembering that it's completely normal for kids of elementary-school age to be careless about possessions, whether they have one home or two. You may be able to cut down on the inconvenience of having possessions left at the other house by helping your child make and routinely use a checklist of sports equipment, musical instruments, bicycles, and other items that travel back and forth regularly.
- Avoiding escalating problems by being visibly impatient about your ex-spouse's incompetence in mat-

ters you were formerly responsible for. Men may
have problems with cooking and housekeeping routines, for example, and women may be unable to do
bicycle repair.

- Being prepared to accept the fact that not all your
time arrangements will always be fair. If things
work out well on a monthly or yearly basis, and the
kids are humming along well, be grateful.
- Using positive language when communicating dis-
appointments. "I was worried about your late return. I'd really appreciate a quick call when you
know you're running late," or "Please remember to
bring Dana's homework back. I'm glad she was able
to share it with you."
- Being flexible when the other parent becomes sick,
grandparents drop in from out of town, or your
planned activity interferes with the other's schedule.
- Asking children for input about schedules. They
may come up with ideas that can solve your problem.
- Seeing a family counselor for help in implementing
these new arrangements if you're having trouble.

With time, a workable pattern emerges on its own and
emotional transitions between homes will happen
smoothly and instantly. And after you've settled into a
comfortable routine, it will probably change! Change
can come through specific discussions based on your
family's changing needs, or it may come informally,
without your ever formalizing the changes.

As your children reach the teen years, you may find
that you and your former spouse both lose access to
them as their peers become important. Don't be hurt if
your child responds with, "I love you—but I'd rather
be with Jason this weekend." This is normal, but it is
still important to let a teenager know which parent he
or she should be checking in with so one of you is still
accountable for that child.

IF IT ISN'T IMPORTANT ENOUGH
TO MATTER A YEAR FROM NOW,
IT ISN'T IMPORTANT ENOUGH
TO ARGUE ABOUT TODAY.

—Carole J. Pierce

The "Transfer" Maneuver

Transferring children is a part of any divorce. It is an even more frequent and important part of shared parenting. Remember to:

- Remind your child 15 to 30 minutes before they can be expected to be picked up.
- Don't use drop-off or pickup time to discuss volatile issues with your ex.
- Avoid upset and conflict with a child just prior to pickup time.
- Pick your child up at the other parent's house when your time begins. It eliminates the sadness for the other parent that comes with dropping them off when they switch homes. It can also establish a routine so that you're never in doubt as to who's responsible for the pickup or drop-off.
- Be punctual about pickups. The tension of lateness takes its toll on the waiting child.
- Let your child assume a degree of accountability for possessions. If an item is forgotten, then it just stays at the other house.
- Develop a routine for beginning and ending each visit, such as always stopping at the same restaurant or sharing a favorite snack on the way home.
- Smooth the way for a child having trouble with a transition time by saying, "I know it's hard for you to say good-bye to one of us and say hello to the other at the same time."

- Be aware that if a child seems to be pulling away from you toward the end of a visit, it is likely that he or she is preparing for the transition between homes—not rejecting you.
- Telephone a waiting parent when you realize you're running late. It's a courtesy that establishes trust.
- Honk, knock, or ring the doorbell—but don't just walk in on your former spouse when you do arrive.

Be specific and consistent in your schedules; after a while you won't remember it any other way.

If you and your former spouse aren't on cordial terms, there is an added strain on these times. You might want to try some of these options:

- Arrange not to be around.
- Have pickups or drop-offs at a friend's or relative's.
- Use school, or day care, as your place of transition.

Unfortunately even anger managed this way puts added stress on kids.

Being in the same school district is a definite advantage. It gives the kids the option of getting off the school bus at either house so neither parent has the pickup responsibility.

When I have custody for the week, I simply pick up the children from their after-school care center on Friday. This gives us the weekend to have fun before the demanding weekly routine begins. It also eliminates contact with my ex and the impression that either of us is taking the children away from the other. —Sandra Pope, LA, CA

Transitions for Parents

In addition to what it involves for the children, joint physical custody also means that *YOU* are not a parent for a sizable amount of your time. You don't realize how much of your parenting role becomes part of your self-definition and structures your time until you divorce and become a part-time parent. You may begin to feel a bit schizophrenic as you swing from single person to parent person and back. The transition from parenting to private time can be surprisingly painful. Sometimes you may even find yourself withdrawing from your kids even before they leave to reduce the pain of their departure. (This should make you more sympathetic to them when they "act out" upon departure or arrival.) Make the transition easier on yourself by planning for your off-time:

- Use the time for taking a class or visiting with friends.
- Keep a running list of things you want to do but haven't had the time for—letters to write, a museum to visit, or a special book to read.
- Develop your own transition rituals, such as a long bath when you are finally alone.
- If you haven't already, begin to keep a journal. Record your feelings of loneliness or observations about your children's progress now that you have time to get some perspective on them.
- Clean the kids' rooms and then keep a light on in them. Or clean their rooms just before they return to ease yourself back into your parenting role.
- Plan your time before the kids depart.

Eventually, a natural pattern will emerge, but don't allow that lonely emptiness to swallow you up. You'll find that just when you've gotten used to being alone, you will again have the reentry problem of returning to your parenting role.

GOOD MANNERS ARE MADE UP
OF PETTY COMPROMISES.

—Emerson

8

Looking Down the Road

DIVORCE IS A PROCESS, NOT A SINGLE EVENT.

This is not an original statement; it has been stated by many others who have written on the subject. It bears repeating, though, because it is worth remembering as we move through every step from the decision to separate to the realization that we have, at last, settled comfortably into our new lives. And it may be comforting to realize that you are not alone. According to the 1984 U.S. Census, nearly 26 percent of all American families have only one parent in the household.

The first year is often the most unsettled, the most chaotic. Most divorced parents find the second year easier. But life always changes; neither your world nor that of your children is ever static. New routines are adapted. Adjustment is made to financial conditions. Traditions are set up gradually, and family holiday celebrations are modified. You have time to nurture new friendships that were not possible when you were married.

Single and separate parenting is something you get better at with time and practice.

LONG-TERM ADJUSTMENTS

There are really two periods of adjustment following a separation and divorce. The information presented here focuses more on your immediate concerns and reactions of the first weeks, months, and your initial year of adjustment. This does not mean that it will all be smooth sailing after that. Even if the custodial arrangements were constant when the children were younger, there will probably be changes in these arrangements during adolescent years. You will need to be flexible.

Your restructured family will shift into a second stage of adjustment (and maybe later a third and fourth) with time and new circumstances. Each will bring with it new reactions and concerns that must be dealt with as they arise. Time will not heal every wound— and even when a wound heals, a scar often remains. It's normal to be hesitant to love and trust. No one wants to be *that* vulnerable again. But frequently we do fall in love again and hopefully are just a bit wiser for it all.

ALL FAMILIES EVOLVE AND
RESTRUCTURE OVER TIME.

IT'S NOT WHAT YOU SAY TO
PEOPLE BUT WHAT THEY HEAR
THAT COUNTS.

—John Powell

As for the loneliness, there is no way out of it but through it. After all, we face all of the toughest things in life alone—from being born, to dying, from loving to feeling pain.

I don't mind being alone but I am lonely. But I was lonely in my marriage, too.
                    —*Mother of two, separated six months*

When It's Finally Final

Despite the relief, the day your divorce is final is yet another emotional milestone. It's hard to know how you will react until the time comes. Consider inviting a friend with you or to join you for lunch afterward, if a court appearance is required. If you're taking time off from a job you may or may not want to go back to work. Keep your options open. Sometimes you aren't aware of your official divorce date until the papers arrive, your lawyer contacts you, or you read it in the newspaper. In any case:

- Mark the occasion. Don't let it slide by or pretend it's not a major day. You don't have to celebrate. Perhaps just eat out, say a special bedtime prayer, or light candles to signify a new beginning.
- Consider letting your children read a copy of your decree (with the dollar figures eliminated) so that they know what the terms are.
- Explain clearly if there will be changes in their lives now that the decree is final.

I have had to show my oldest child a copy of our divorce decree several times so she understood why she had more days at Dad's house.
                    —*Rod Martel, Minneapolis, MN*

Even believing your marriage failed and talking about it provides a description of a marriage. When the marriage becomes a memory, part of your history—it will no longer be a marriage.

LIFE IS A PROCESS OF LOSING OUR ILLUSIONS.

On a practical level, remember to think about your will. Guardianship of your children and your assets are now new considerations that should be dealt with at once, especially if you are the sole custodian. If this wasn't part of your divorce decree, it's time to go back to your lawyer and have something on paper. Lack of planning can necessitate new custody battles and put children of deceased single parents in limbo for months. Discuss your arrangements and wishes with the appropriate parties so as one lawyer said, "Everyone knows who will take the children home from the funeral."

We were concerned about how we would cope with the death of the other parent. We agreed that while the children were young, we'd each keep a life insurance policy with the other parent as beneficiary to help with expenses in the event of death.

—Unsigned

What's In a Name?

Many women choose to return to their maiden name after divorce. This can be done legally or just as a de facto act. This decision is always a very personal one; what's right for you is what feels right. Even so, as your children's mother, there will always be times when you should probably refer to yourself by your married name for ease of identification, even if you do choose to drop your married name in the normal course of your day.

Changing your name *legally* is not difficult but it takes a bit more paperwork. You can do it as part of your divorce decree or you can do it later yourself. You will need to fill out an application for a name change and schedule a courtroom hearing, which usually is a brief procedure. There are fees involved at each step, but it is not a complicated process.

I took my maiden name back at the time of my divorce. For me it was an affirmation of my personal integrity. It was amusing that my kids asked if they could, too! I told them I didn't think that would work real well.
— Jean Travis, Bloomington, MN

TAKING CARE OF YOURSELF

After the divorce paperwork is completed, you must work on your inner divorce. Sometimes that's the bigger job. Coming to grips with your own anger is important. In the beginning anger has a useful purpose; it allows you to distance yourself from your former spouse. But continuing anger requires creative, constructive expression. Revenge must be processed intellectually. Verbalizing venom with trusted friends or in counseling is important and useful, but *children are never suitable recipients of your fury.* You'll only be "done" with your anger when you're tired of hearing your own war stories, when you no longer have to let another know the *real* scoop, and when you can finally see your former partner as a benign friend, stranger, or distant relative.

To help you get through your "inner divorce":

- If you haven't already done so, start a journal to record your feelings and your daily progress. It's for your eyes only. Don't worry about writing well; just get the words down on paper. Keeping track of the sequence of events for later reference or describing your ex's behavior or your anger can be healthful when vented here. (Down the road, a long way down, it can be a valuable legacy for your children to read when they reach adulthood.)
- Find other acceptable ways to release tension and strong emotions. Take up a new sport or relearn an old favorite.
- Take care of your body. Eat regular and balanced meals, and get enough rest and exercise. Indulge yourself with a new hairstyle or a membership at a tennis club. Don't let your distress be an excuse for excess eating or drinking; no one will be hurt but you.
- Get a massage, if your budget allows. The lack of touch, if you have been used to it, can be very hard.
- Be more careful around the house, when walking outside, and especially while driving. Accidents are more likely to occur when you are preoccupied and upset. Divorcing people have a higher than usual incidence of traffic violations.
- Understand that if you are not experienced in thinking for yourself or valuing yourself separately from your marital relationship, taking responsibility may seem even harder. Rest assured that over time, your newfound self-reliance will amaze and delight you.
- If you have money to invest, remember the words of Caroline Donnelly of *Money* magazine: "Nobody, not your broker, your accountant or your brother-in-

law will care or worry as much about your money as you do. There is no single best investment, and there's nothing wrong with simple, conservative investments that let you sleep at night. You'll earn more money by spending your energy on your career than on your investments and if you live within your means by a wide enough margin, budgeting is unnecessary."

- Attend a support group. Sharing experiences with others who have "been there" lessens the pain.
- Select a friend or relative (*not* an in-law) with whom you can share your feelings. Sound out your perspectives for decision making. Don't overburden your friend, though, and be prepared to return the favor.
- Examine your attitude toward the opposite sex. If you are bitter—and remain that way—you are likely to color your children's lives in lasting ways.
- Get counseling. No one should or has to "tough this one out." If you weren't angry before, I promise you the process will make you so. Don't store this emotional baggage. It will sink you.

YOU CAN'T GO BACK, ESPECIALLY IF YOU WEREN'T THE ONE WHO LEFT.

Separation and divorce produce a great deal of stress that affects the body's immune system. A study at the Ohio University College of Medicine compared women who had been separated from their husbands for less than a year with women who were still married. Blood tests showed that separated women had lower levels of cells that resist tumors and bacteria and higher levels of cells that indicated a susceptibility to virus. (The study also showed that marital conflict itself takes

a toll on one's health.) And, grief, including the grief
experienced in a divorce, is physically as well as emotionally exhausting. The fatigue you feel is the body's
way of processing emotional stress. Treat yourself with
extra TLC, especially when your body is sending you
obvious signals. If you don't know how to nurture
yourself, consider talking to a counselor. Time, restructuring your life, and finding new ways to bring
happiness into your life will therefore be your best
prescription for a healthier you. And beyond access to
both parents and the ending of parental conflicts, the
well-being of the care-taking parent often determines
the adjustment of the children.

---

*Divorce was the hardest thing I've ever done. Even though
it was a choice I had made (after fifteen years), I was not
prepared for the pain.*
                                    —Linda Wiesman, Elizabethtown, NJ

Dealing with the Pain

If we only knew just how long it will take for the
inner pain (which more often feels like panic) to go
away, we could just settle in and wait. Instead we live
with an inner roller-coaster over which we have no
control. Just when you think you have got a handle on
your feelings, you nose-dive again. It is important that
you remember (from the voices of experience) that
these peaks and valleys do become less steep and the
ride will smooth out—but it's never done on our schedule, and it always seems to take longer than we would
like or allot time for.

When the pain hits:

• Go for a walk. Do something physical.
• Write down your thoughts and feelings on paper.

- Call a friend.
- Call an acquaintance who you think might become a friend.
- Remember every divorced person has felt like you do now and lived through it. Eventually it will become part of your past.

I found that walking the exact route on my daily walk became important. A cousin told me she swam laps because it was important to her that she could only go as far as the end of the pool. I guess self-imposed boundaries and routines can be therapeutic for adults as well as kids.

—Unsigned

Reading Relief

Pick up a piece of insightful reading. It really does help, especially on weekends and at bedtime. The following three books are well known and widely recommended. They can all be read in bits and pieces. Concentration during divorce, you may have noticed, is no small task.

- *How to Survive the Loss of a Love*, by Colgrove, Bloomfield, and McWilliams (Bantam, 1977). A short collection of easy-to-read prose by a psychologist, psychiatrist, and a poet, for overcoming emotional hurts.
- *No Hidden Meanings*, by Sheldon Kopp (Science and Behavior Press, 1975). A photo essay of a list of "truths" that originally appeared in his book, *If You Meet Budda on the Road, Kill Him*. They are profound sentences relevant to the human condition that can keep life in perspective.

- **Divorce: The Pain and the Healing,* by Judith Mattison (Augsburg, 1985). This collection of sensitive meditations on the end of this author's marriage will strike a chord with your hurt feelings. It will help with the healing process needed during this process of crisis, separation, and readjustment.

*See page 244.

GUILT AND BLAME AND ALL THAT

Parenting and guilt go together like peanut butter and jelly. The parental guilt that follows divorce is monumental—and just as futile as the guilt you felt the first time you lost your temper and spanked your child. Divorce feels like failure, and failure feels bad. Don't heap all the guilt and responsibility on yourself. Blaming your ex-spouse is just as bad—and just as useless.

Fighting Back Against All That

All parents think to some degree that through the breakup of their marriage they have failed their kids. It helps to recognize that your feelings of grief, rage, and depression are perfectly normal after a divorce. Do the best you can taking care of yourself and the kids, if they're with you, as you work through your feelings. Don't allow yourself the "luxury" of self-pity, because that usually turns into guilt for thinking you are selfish. What *will* work is:

- Giving up trying to be mother and father to make up for one less parent being around. Being just one parent is fine. Look for others (such as friends, relatives, teachers, etc.) to help meet your child's needs for other adults.

- Being careful to avoid role-reversal while you resolve your old grievances and start to pick up the pieces. Some parents find they are especially prone to lean on children of the opposite sex, looking on them as "the man of the family" or "a good little housekeeper." Kids need to be kids; they need to know parents will be parents.
- Trying to remember that much of the negative behavior your children may display—including many of their problems—is just part of their growing up and not necessarily the result of the divorce. One phase will replace another, just as it did in your old family life.
- Not apologizing to your child for getting divorced. Your divorce was not set up to hurt your child intentionally.
- Learning to tolerate your children's disapproval of your setting and enforcing limits. Tolerating rejection without another adult backing you up is hard, but that's what is required of you as a single parent.
- Trying to not make up to the kids for the divorce by devoting yourself entirely to them. You are entitled to a life of your own, and if you don't have it, you'll risk becoming a martyr and a stifling, dull, overpro-

---

I felt so guilty about my divorce depriving my children of a "normal" family that I did nothing for myself for the first five years after the separation. All I did was work to support them and stay home to take care of them. I didn't realize how bad this was for them until one by one, each of the older children moved to California to be with their dad and away from their dull, martyrish mother.

—Unsigned

tective parent. And that will create another kind of guilt later.

- Refusing to indulge in excessive material items or guilt trips (the "nothing-is-too-good-for-my-child" syndrome) or deprive yourself to give your children "more."
- Not saying yes to your child's every whim. It will produce a demanding, self-centered child who believes you owe him or her any and every compensation for your divorce.
- Knowing what you know about guilt, being careful not to encourage your kids to feel guilty about loving and enjoying being with their other parent. Let them know you have plans and that you'll be okay while they are gone.
- Avoiding supermomism or superdadism. Remind yourself that you are doing the best you can—which is all any of us can do.

And if you are experiencing that most guilt-laden trip of all—resenting having kids at all (or having the major responsibility for them)—be gentle on yourself. We've all found ourselves with that feeling at one time or another.

Legally I was a single woman but I did not feel single. I always had my two children in my life to whom I felt bound. Then I would feel guilty.

—Lynn Gail, Boston, MA

THE WORKING PARENT

The breadwinner/homemaker/parent combination most divorced parents with sole or shared custody assume is a physical, emotional, and financial struggle. The change occurs abruptly; a father or mother must assume most of the responsibility for the children, permanently or for a time, without adequate time to prepare. Men who have not shared household and parenting chores equally—and this means many men—find it hard to learn how to run a house and deal with kids' emotional needs in addition to earning a living. (The movie *Kramer Versus Kramer* is one popular example of a man's learning experience—although it reinforces stereotypes of males as initially incompetent.) Women returning to the work force after several years at home, or entering it for the first time, find themselves exhausted and overwhelmed. The main problem for many women is that of money; a drop in their standard of living is almost a given.

According to Faye Smith, a psychologist at Smith College, divorce interferes with work more than any other trauma in a person's life. During the first three months after a spouse walks out, the other spouse (male or female) is usually virtually incapable of focusing on work. Once the reality of divorce is accepted, it is possible to regain one's attention span.

Attitude Counts

Although it's tough:

- Refuse to feel guilty about having to work, and don't be apologetic about it. Study after study has proven that children do not necessarily suffer either emotionally or intellectually because they live with single parents who work outside their homes.

- Be aware that your own attitude about working is the strongest factor in your children's acceptance of the situation. They won't resent your job if you don't; they won't feel envious of friends who have a home-based parent if you don't bemoan your fate.
- Involve the kids in your job in whatever ways you can. Let them visit you at your workplace, if possible, or at least see the building and meet some of the people you spend your working hours with.
- Leave work at work. Make the hours you spend with the kids count by giving them your full attention and doing things together that you all enjoy.
- Let your school-aged child know about the restrictions your job will put on your participation in school events. Let him or her have a voice in selecting which activities you will be able to attend or assist with.
- Build into your budget some minor indulgences, such as meals out, movies, trips to places of interest. Remember that kids need a parent, not a Santa Claus. Breakfast in a restaurant is as much fun as dinner, and it will cost less. An afternoon at the roller skating rink may be more enjoyable for everyone than attendance at a costly theater production.
- Invest in a pager if it fits your work, life-style, and need to be accessible to your kids.

Many parents also throw themselves into their jobs, especially during times they don't have their children. It's a satisfying and good short-term coping mechanism to escape the pain. Many women, especially, are often forced into long working hours out of economic necessity. Often, keeping work in perspective is not easy.

The hardest is when you're in an important meeting at work and can't leave and the school calls about your sick child. Those are the days when I feel like I'm wearing a sign that reads "good career woman—bad mother." These do get balanced out, fortunately, by the times I do stay home with my child and feel the guilt of "bad career woman—good mother."

—Susan Beatty, New Canaan, CT

Making Time When There Is None

Life goes on. Laundry has to be done, food must be shopped for—and all with less time than you probably had available to you before. Your emotional paralysis and the counseling you are attending will limit your time and resources even more. Just as when your children were first born, some things just won't get done—for now. Remember, no one "has it all," so:

- Set up a schedule for household chores and errands, delegating whatever tasks the kids are able to handle. Keep it loose enough to allow for the emergencies that will surely arise. And be flexible enough to throw that schedule to the wind once in awhile and do something unexpected and fun.
- Use chore lists and written messages as two of your best organizational tools.
- Consider having a live-in student or boarder, hiring a mother's helper or housekeeper to ease your time limitations and add some continuity to everyone's life. For some, communal arrangements (a la TV's "Kate and Allie") work.
- Take time to set your priorities. Do the "musts" and let the "shoulds" and "coulds" wait until you have time.

- Use the phone or the mail for shopping whenever you can. Run errands as infrequently as possible, combining them into a single trip.
- Relax your standards about housework and cooking. It's not important right now that your house be immaculate at all times and your meals all of gourmet quality. A study from the East Carolina University in Greenville, North Carolina, found that divorced mothers spend as much time with their children—and sometimes more—than when they were married. How? They spend less time on housework and personal leisure.
- If the other parent has the kids part of the time, let those be the days or weeks you catch up on work around the house—but also those in which you spend some time on yourself or with friends.
- Develop friendships with other single parents with whom you can trade or share in transportation and child-care areas.

WE CANNOT MAKE LIFE EASIER.
WE CAN ONLY MAKE
OURSELVES STRONGER.

SCHOOL, KIDS, AND DIVORCE

The effects of divorce on behavior and school performance differ from child to child. Some have a very hard time, fail academically, ignore teachers' and counselors' efforts to help, refuse to participate in anything not required, and lose friends because of belligerence or apathy. It's really because school is hard to manage when you're grieving and in pain. Other children look upon school as a lifesaver. They become immersed in studies, activities, and friendships as an escape. Some even find the chance to talk with teachers, counselors, or friends about the divorce a way to unload; others may prefer to keep family problems at home and look upon school as a place to relax and forget them.

Teachers will assume kids live with both parents unless they are told otherwise. So tell them what the situation is and let your child know you will be informing his or her teacher. That doesn't mean your child will be happy that you're letting their teachers know. In fact, don't be surprised if they are angry—initially—because of their own sensitivity and embarrassment. Still it avoids minor discomfort for teacher and child during the school year. Be sensitive to the personality of your child's teacher. Not all will be sympathetic. If necessary, choose a counselor, nurse, secretary, or anyone you know there who is most likely to be helpful to your child. The sooner you do this, the better.

My first reaction was to keep it a "secret." But it was only one week before my son's preschool teacher asked if anything had changed at home. He had become inattentive and bully-ish. I realized I had to enlist their help so he could cope better. They did and he did.
—Karyn Herrmann, Minneapolis, MN

Children of Divorce in the Classroom

The good news is that a child of divorce is definitely not an oddity in a classroom today. He or she has plenty of company. It's not unusual to find 40 to 50 percent of children in a classroom have experienced divorce in their families. Peer pressure or the stigma of the "D word" will not be an issue. Regardless, children may feel self-conscious, isolated, and embarrassed.

There's often some bad news in the beginning. Children are, of course, upset by the trauma of divorce in the family. Their lives are changed and there are bound to be some initial problems in school as well as at home. A 1986 study by Dr. John Guidubaldi at Kent State University found that lack of structure at home and fears about financial security are seen as the major reasons that children of divorce have more problems in school than do other children. Stress from home usually affects a child's ability to concentrate. Kids will daydream, be inattentive, and may have trouble completing assignments. Parents who are alert to signs of trouble can often help a child make a quick adjustment to life at school through discussions, changes in their parental behavior, or with professional help.

In general, children in single-parent families do not do as well in school as their intact-family counterparts. But other studies have shown that the kids of divorced parents don't necessarily have continuing problems in school, though for some reason, boys are more likely to be classified as "low achievers" than those from intact families. Mothers who worry about returning to work will find comfort in knowing latchkey children do as well as others academically, and often become more independent and resourceful as well.

If your school or PTA offers student group counseling sessions during school hours, encourage your child's participation. Kids benefit from hearing others experiencing their feelings and from having a place to vent their own. If your school doesn't have such a project available but is open to the idea, contact Charmaine Rusu, Echo Mountain PTA, 1811 E. Michigan Ave., Phoenix, Arizona 85022, for information on starting one. Or you can contact Elizabeth McGonagol, Wood Road Elementary School, Wood Road, Ballston Spa,

New York 12020, for a manual on another model program called "Banana Splits: A Peer Support Program for the Survivors of Divorce Wars."

Rights of the Noncustodial Parent

For many parents, the communication line to school is severed by separation. One parent no longer has automatic access to a child's school life. Even with generous custody arrangements, there is usually an information gap so that one parent is at the mercy of the child's memory or the goodwill of the other parent.

Society is recognizing that divorced fathers have both rights and responsibilities in connection with their children, particularly under joint custody. The Family Education Rights Act of 1974 gives the noncustodial parent access to pertinent records. The Federal District Court in Albany, New York, in 1985 upheld a father with joint custody's request to receive duplicate copies of all school information mailed to his former wife, who had custody on school days. The decision did not cover handouts the children carried home. Prior to that, his only recourse was the federal law that does mandate that schools make a child's grades available to both parents, no matter what kind of custodial arrangements have been made.

To help take the pressure off a child:

- Begin sharing and talking about school decisions immediately to avoid setting up a noninvolvement pattern.
- Be very careful to pass copies of school information and report cards from one joint-custody parent to another when a child changes homes, so that the parent in charge is aware of special happenings. Request that routine school notices, newsletters, and

other information that's mailed be sent to both
parents.

- Be sure the school has phone numbers and addresses (work and home) for both parents in their
files. Both phone numbers should also be listed in
the school student directory, even if you wish to
list just one address.
- Remember to include examples of schoolwork when
your child packs to go to the other parent's home.
- Encourage your child to share good school news
with the other parent by phone.
- Arrange pickups by a noncustodial parent or changes
from residence between parents with joint custody
in a way that causes the minimum of disturbance.
Teachers have noted that Mondays and Fridays,
when changes of residence have either just taken
place or are about to occur, are often harder days
for some children of divorced parents.

Consider joining the PTA yourself. It's a good way of
staying in touch and involved. Unfortunately, come
graduation there is often a limit of two tickets per
family and compromises or separate seating options
must be made if you can't tolerate your ex-spouse's
company on such a nice occasion.

School Conferences

Make every effort to attend parent-teacher conferences—either together or separately. Teachers are making time for those *extra* conferences if parents are just
too uncomfortable together. Ask for a time change if
you cannot meet during school hours. Don't hesitate to
request additional meetings whenever you feel they're
necessary. Even in the midst of your pain, you might
be surprised to see how nice it feels to talk with a
third party about your wonderful child. Relationship

and money concerns can be put aside and you and your ex can enjoy the good thing (your kids) that you do have in common. At the very least, set up school as neutral territory. Don't turn an open house into an open confrontation.

We tried a shared conference and it was a disaster. The teacher offered us separate conferences the next time and it was helpful and beneficial for our son, too.
— Karyn Herrmann, Minneapolis, MN

Our shared conference went well. We also used this time to inform some of the teachers of the divorce.
— Toni Richardson, Hopkins, MN

Make sure that your child understands that although joint conferences are a shared parenting responsibility of adults, they are only that. Children having reconciliation fantasies often "act out" at school, knowing that Mom and Dad will respond by going to school together.

It's up to parents to supply the details that will allow school personnel to do their best. Conferences are the place to fill in the teachers if you have not done so before. You don't want to put your child's teachers in an embarrassing situation when they say, "Ask your father," who may live 1,000 miles away or when they address a stepfather incorrectly.

Keep your school informed:

- Ask to be contacted about problems or behavioral changes.
- Check to see whether the school offers counseling services or classes.

- Let the teacher know whether to contact one parent or both.
- Advise teachers of your custody schedule in general so they will be understanding of any glitches that may occur.

After-School and Extracurricular Activities

Regardless of your custodial arrangements there will be after-school activities that your child will want both parents to attend, whether soccer, Little League, Open House, or the class play. The first few times are the hardest but you—and all the neighbors—will soon get used to seeing you (a) talking to each other at these events, (b) not talking to each other at these events, (c) sitting together, (d) sitting or standing at opposite ends of a stadium or arena, (e) bringing along a significant other, (f) never bringing along your significant other, or (g) alternating events so that you never show up at the same ones together. It doesn't matter which of these options you choose, but it is important that you do show up, for your child's sake. It's sometimes difficult, but it gets easier if you work at it.

I don't think you ever lose the "radar" that lets you spot your former spouse across a field of 500 parents. But, conversely, your child will never miss seeing you there (i.e., both parents) if you do show up. These same kids will *always* remember if you don't.

FAMILY ADJUSTMENTS

Among the most important and most difficult adjustments a divorced parent must make are those that concern personal relationships. First, of course, are those with the children. Then there's the former spouse—the other parent. You'll always be connected to your ex through your children. The better you can manage a new kind of partnership, the more the children will benefit.

Then there are the grandparents. As well as having a right to two parents, your children have a right to two sets of grandparents, if they're living and if there's no real reason why they should be avoided. (Most grandparents feel they have a right to their grandchildren, too, no matter what the circumstances of the divorce, and they're beginning to be quite vocal about their feelings.) Other members of the family have to be considered, too—siblings, cousins, aunts, and uncles on both sides of the family. If you've been close to all those folks and seen much of them, there is bound to be a certain awkwardness, if not real problems during and after a divorce. At best, those great gatherings on holidays are probably over, and your close friendship with your husband's sister or your wife's brother becomes strained. Unfortunately, the two sides of the family often split down the middle, siding with "their own." The answer for many divorced parents is to find or create a new extended family, a support group made up of old and/or new friends who share some of the same kinds of experiences and are available to help in emergencies.

All single-parent families do not come in one flavor— weak. There are as many varieties as among two-parent families.

—Ellen Goodman, The Boston Globe

Grandparents, and the "Other" Grandparents

Divorce dramatically and quickly changes the role of grandparents, so naturally they will have their own adjustments to make. Sometimes they are called upon for financial aid, for temporary housing, for baby-sitting services, and are expected to give advice only when asked for it. Grandchildren may disappear from their lives or take over their lives. Your divorce is not just your divorce—it's theirs, too.

The perfect grandparents give kids a sense of continuity and the awareness of belonging to a large and interesting family. They're always available to love a child and to listen, and kids sometimes find it easier to confide in them than in a parent. The elders can also fill in for an absent parent, giving him or her the gift of time off without worry. Of course, not all grandparents measure up to that ideal. Even your own parents may disappoint you by withholding their support or by siding with your spouse. Or, with the best intentions in the world, they may begin to treat you like a child and try to assume some of your responsibilities. Your in-laws may be even less helpful, siding totally with their own adult child. They may be militant about their rights as grandparents. They may try to turn your own children against you. In the event of sole custody or conflicting loyalties they may ignore your children because they're "yours."

Your relationship with the "other" grandparents *will* change. That doesn't mean it has to be bad or good, only that it will be somewhat different. The form that difference takes will only emerge with time. Grandparents are unsure of their role after divorce. Their choosing to remain neutral may seem like a "lack of caring" to you. It's important to keep family ties intact:

- Deal with your own parents as logically and compassionately as you can. If they've been supportive and helpful before, and seem not to be now, they'll probably come around once they realize your divorce is real and you still love and need them. Parents have to deal with their own embarrassment and sense of loss.
- Give them time to deal with their own emotions and disappointment. Remember, they weren't consulted about your divorce.
- Make the first move—and the second, if necessary—toward keeping your in-laws in your children's lives, if not your own. The worst that can happen is that you will be turned down, and in that case, you'll know you've tried.
- Consider going the extra mile if you wish to continue the relationship with the former in-laws for the kids' sake, and try again after a cooling-off period of a few weeks or months. Time heals; circumstances change.
- Don't allow yourself to feel guilty if the hostility continues and the relationship ends completely. It may actually be best in the long run, and kids will eventually realize that, although they may be hurt at first.
- Be willing to listen to the grandparents on both sides if they need to unload their feelings about you and your former spouse's failings. Don't use them as your confidants, though. Keep them out of the middle.
- Never threaten to cut your children off from their grandparents; doing so will only heat up unnecessary battles.

Kids can get caught in the loyalty binds between parent and grandparent just like they can between parent and parent. Watch your words.

Senior Resources

Grandparents'-Children's Rights, Inc.
5728 Bayonne Ave.
Haslett, MI 48840
517-339-8663
An organization concerned with safeguarding grandparents' visiting rights in cases of divorce, death, and abuse; a clearinghouse for information pertaining to state laws and pending legislation across the country.

The Foundation for Grandparents/ Arthur Kornhaber
35 Riverside Drive
Lake Placid, NY 12946
Promotes expectant grandparent programs in hospitals around the country and sponsors a summer camp for grandparents and grandchildren in the Adirondacks.

Grandparents Anonymous
1924 Beverly
Sylvan Lake, MI 48053
313-682-8384
For grandparents who are denied legal visitation with grandchildren as a result of divorce or a breakdown in family communications.

Or read *What to Do When Your Son or Daughter Divorces*, by Inez Gottlieb, Dorothy W. Gottlieb, and Marjorie A. Slavin (Bantam, 1988).

SINGLE PARENTS AND HOLIDAYS

The more importance your family has attached to holidays and the more elaborate your preparations have been, the harder it will be to break traditions and make drastic changes. Unless your ex-spouse has pulled away entirely from the family, he or she will undoubt-

edly spend some holidays with the children and you
will be alone for some of them. Plan for those days as
carefully as you do for the ones when the kids are
with you. Try to make them as different from the old
days as possible—visit friends in another town, go on
a skiing or hiking trip with other single people, do
something you've never done before.

The first holidays with your new family structure
are the most difficult, whether your children are with
you or their other parent. That's the bad news. The
good news is there is only one first time for each
holiday. You'll survive each "first," and it will get
better each succeeding year. Small comfort, I know.
Turning the lemons into lemonade takes a bit of planning and effort. Don't carry the burden alone; share
feelings with your children if they are old enough and
let them help with your plans. And if they feel their
own sadness, let them voice these feelings, too, for
they are normal.

Dividing the Holidays

Consider every possibility before you settle on the
holiday divisions that work best for you. It's logical
that the kids spend Mother's day with Mom, Father's
Day with Dad, and visit for respective birthdays. But
there is also July 4th, Labor Day, Memorial Day, and
President's Day to think about. Other big days (Easter
or Passover, Christmas or Chanukah, and Thanksgiv-
ing) are a bit harder to handle. Some divorced parents
alternate holidays each year, others divide the more
important ones, alternating even this division from
year to year. Keep in mind that for a holiday like
Christmas, waiting "until next year" to celebrate with
Mom or Dad is a very long wait for children. In some
families it works best if the children spend certain

religious holidays with the parent who is most involved with church or synagogue.

Examine your holiday traditions. You may discover
that you have continued to do things you don't like
just because you have always done them. Now is a
good time to make changes:

* Make decisions about "who gets whom" and "who
  goes where" as far ahead as possible, and tell the
  children so they will know what they are doing.
  Ask teenagers for their input, keeping in mind that
  they may want to spend some of their holiday time
  with friends—without either parent. A well-planned
  schedule is especially important the first year.
* Celebrate the eve of the holiday at one home and
  the day of the holiday at the other. Children often
  like this best because they get double the holiday
  fun, which makes up for what they have lost in
  family unity.
* Consider separating the children so they can share
  the holiday alone with one parent. You can switch
  midway through (if proximity allows) so each child
  has some time with both parents. We often put the
  burden of family togetherness on children by assuming that if they are together at the holidays,
  then at least some part of the family is "intact," but
  children often enjoy being "singletons." Separating
  them is also one way of ensuring that neither parent will be alone.

Children like having both parents together on family
occasions if the parents are comfortable enough in
each other's presence to handle it and are not feeding
into reconciliation fantasies. Perhaps the "gift" of occasional togetherness can work for your family more
easily when it is the child who is being celebrated, as
happens on birthdays. There are ways you can ease

these times, too. Eat out on neutral ground or if your ex is coming over for a family meal, make it a buffet to avoid the problem of who will sit at the head of the table.

I had one Christmas morning without the girls, and I was extremely depressed. His family celebrates Christmas on Christmas Eve so that hasn't happened since. I don't mind them being gone on Christmas Day or any other holiday "day," but I don't like waking up on Christmas or Easter morning without them. Any other holiday is okay.

—Margaret Leduc, Romulus, MI

Holiday Traditions

- Start new traditions. Let your children help you come up with new ideas. Will it be caroling? Visiting grandparents or friends in a nursing home? If you always opened gifts Christmas day, open them on Christmas Eve this year. Make sledding on New Year's Eve a new annual event. The nice thing about "new" is that it doesn't have to mean "less" or "damaged."
- Discuss past celebrations and traditions if the kids want to. Acknowledging these memories validates a child's feeling that it's all right to yearn for or mourn former times. Keeping some traditions and, perhaps modifying them slightly, can provide a sense of continuity and comfort.
- Change the scene, if you can. Spend the holidays someplace you've never been—especially if you won't have the kids with you over the holidays. But do try to go to a place where you won't be alone. That can be depressing. Try to find a friend or relative you can visit or travel with.

- If you can't get away, at least go out to eat and to the movies or do something you enjoy. Have you always wanted to see *The Nutcracker* or *The Little Match Girl* but never got around to it? Do it now! Again, don't go alone if you can help it.
- Coordinate, if possible, gift choices with your ex. Children may be happy with two of the same gift, but you may not be.

Holiday Guidelines and Alternatives

- Be cautious about providing more excitement than the kids are used to, especially younger children. "Two of everything" may make things even, but may also be exhausting. Some parents feel, however, this offsets the "unfairness" kids must tolerate in a divorce and becomes one of the "advantages."
- Be sensitive to grandparents' visiting needs but don't err in the opposite direction by doing everything others expect of you and not meeting your own needs.
- Don't let competitiveness about holiday visits become an undue burden for a child to please a parent, either now—or years down the road.
- Form a support group. With just a little luck, you may find another single parent whose kids are compatible with yours, and you can share holiday meals and celebrations. If you're going to be alone, invite other single parents to join you for Christmas dinner.
- Participate in the activities of your church or synagogue; if you don't belong, join. Don't be afraid to replace previous family ties by tying into a religious community—there is *nothing* hypocritical about it.
- Don't feel guilty about not giving children everything they ask for. They don't need it. One—maybe two—special items won't get lost in the shuffle.

- Don't be apologetic about making drastic changes in gift-giving habits and expensive celebrations if finances are tight. An honest discussion about available dollars will assure a child that cash, not love, is the issue. You will find that children enjoy making gifts and setting up new, less materialistic traditions.
- Above all, be good to yourself. Spend time with your children, perhaps more than you usually do, but save some time and energy for your own hobbies, activities, and friends. The holidays are for everyone—including you.

Be tolerant of the other parent being excessive with gifts. An absent parent will often do this to score points with the kids. Don't interpret this situation as a personal statement against you. Don't let yourself feel competitive or less worthy, if you are less able—or even unwilling—to provide expensive gifts.

I decided we would start a tradition of making cookies and fudge together for Christmas. Christopher talked about the fun we had for weeks.
                              —Karyn Herrmann, Minneapolis, MN

Preparing for Long-Distance Holiday Visits

Holidays are frequently times when children make extended visits to their noncustodial parent's home. Often both parent and child have a fantasy of a perfect visit, which is hard to achieve. It is a good idea to keep to a relaxed pace on a holiday visit and not try to fit a year's activity into one or two weeks. For children, it can be a time of anxiety and ambivalence. They wonder if they will fit in, if they will be welcome, and how it will be to be away from their primary home. If there are new "family" members, how will everyone get along?

You might want to practice some overnights away for a child not used to being away from home. Try a friend who lives close by or a relative's house.

Parents can also reduce previsit tension that children often feel by:

- Being specific about dates and travel plans, with any tickets purchased well in advance.
- Being positive and involved in the visiting preparations—and urging your ex-spouse to do the same.
- Planning on your child taking along some favorite familiar items, from toys and stuffed animals to books, on visits.
- Discussing and planning for phone calls home. Calling home should not be a cause for a child to feel divided loyalties. A child's need to "check in" should not be viewed as a sign of unhappiness with the visit or competition by the parent being visited.
- Preparing personal space for a child so that he or she has a personal "turf."
- Discussing house rules and expectations, which may differ from the other parent's house.
- Preparing a holiday meal, if you are the noncustodial parent, may be more work than you realize. Plan ahead and enlist your children's support and help. Send kids back to their other home with clean clothes and some new items to remember you by.

When it comes to farewell time, remember that a long good-bye hug, wishes for a good visit and trip, and reassurance of your love—as opposed to a teary or bitter send-off—are what children need, no matter whose house they are leaving.

*One twenty-two-year-old woman whose parents were di-
vorced when she was six told me she wept with relief
when she finally spent one Christmas with a friend's
family. It was the first Christmas in sixteen years that
had not included a plane trip, because each parent "loved"
her so much that they wanted to spend at least part of
every Christmas day with her.*

—Unsigned

Traveling Alone By Plane

The airlines are familiar with the large number of
children who are traveling on their own these days
between parents. Are you familiar with their rules
of passage? By age 5, airlines allow children to fly
alone, but:

- Check in early, because there is extra paperwork
  for the gate attendant to fill out. You might also
  want a good choice for seat selections. Windows
  are usually favored.
- Children under the age of 8 are generally permitted only on direct flights. Check with your airline's regulations.
- Be sure the kids have quarters for telephone calls,
  or know how to call collect. Rehearse any other
  possible scenarios that might be appropriate, such
  as what to do if the picking-up party might be
  late.
- You may be billed a service fee for escorting
  children to connecting flights.
- A parent must pay full adult fare for a child
  unless there is a discounted children's fare.
- Let the airline know when you make your reservation that your child will be traveling alone.
- Look around in the boarding area for other kids
  or possible friendly adults who may be willing to

befriend your child en route, even if for only a friendly wave when walking down the aisle during the flight.

- Provide enough items to entertain a child on a flight. There will be no one on board who can attend to or occupy your child. Books, cards, and small toys like magic slates are appropriate. A backpack is the easiest "hand" luggage for kids.
- Your child will not be permitted to listen to a radio headset of his or her own on board because they interfere with plane communications. Audio tape machines (with headsets) are allowed.
- Be prepared to provide the airline and your child with your name, address, and phone number as well as the same information about the person who will be meeting your child.

It's always a good idea to stay in an airport until the plane is actually off the ground. Many boarded planes have been known to disembark because of delays or mechanical difficulties. Also, make "ironclad" arrangements with whoever is picking up the child at the other end, and don't forget the time changes.

BIRTHDAYS

Give careful attention to plans for the kids' birthdays; they're very special days for children. They may be the one celebration both parents find they can share in. If one parent has the party, maybe the other can be a guest or just drop in for a short time. If you're sure this won't work, consider alternating years for the group party and let the parent who does not have the party do something else special.

Gift Giving

Few things are harder to deal with than a child taking a gift you gave him or her to the other parent's house. It's important to bite your tongue in such situations. The fact that children can transport possessions freely between homes is a positive sign of their comfort level with two homes. Don't detract from that. If you are the noncustodial parent, give gifts that will last to keep you remembered to your child. That doesn't mean they should be extravagant. In fact, it's not a good idea to set yourself up as the indulgent parent. Elaborate and expensive gifts aren't good for kids, and they flame the fire of discontent in the heart of your former spouse, who may not be able to give something of equivalent value. Instead, try:

- Magazine subscriptions of your child's choice and interest level as a way to "connect" monthly.
- Sending flowers for a birthday, or to mark any occasion. This appeals to girls of any age.
- If you're in a quandary about what to give, ask your child or your former spouse.
- If you want to give an expensive gift, consider having the other parent be part of the decision to lessen the hostility and competition.

Give gifts when they are due. Timeliness is almost as important as the gifts themselves. A gift a month late tells your child that he or she is not really that important to you. And don't give teenagers expensive gifts if you haven't given them basic support for other things that are important to them; it only breeds hostility.

One friend told of her college-age son asking his dad if he would mind returning the $100 pen set he had given him for Christmas and instead give him a check for the same amount, which the son needed for rent. His dad agreed, took the pen set, but so far has not sent him the check.

—Unsigned

THE BEST GIFT YOU CAN GIVE YOUR CHILDREN IS TO LAY CLAIM TO YOUR OWN LIFE.

MOTHER'S DAY AND FATHER'S DAY

Certain days of the year can be especially painful for divorced parents, but most often for the noncustodial parent. For the father, who is most often the noncustodial parent, Father's Day can be especially difficult. Even if he spends the day with his children, he is reminded that he does not play the same role in his children's lives as he did before. Whereas these holidays were formerly spent as a family holiday, the mother on Father's Day and the father on Mother's Day will now be on their own. If you haven't thought about this ahead of time and made plans of your own, it can be quite a sad day when you are the "other" parent. You might be fortunate enough to have your parents nearby to share the day.

I sent flowers to my wife on Mother's Day after we had been separated for six months. Despite the fact that she initiated the separation and I was still dealing with the pain from that, I wanted to show my appreciation to her for being the mother of our children. And she is a wonderful mother to them. She was touched, and I'm glad I did it.

—Walt Tornow, Plymouth, MN

I invited all the single and divorcing women I knew to my house on my first Father's Day alone—a day I was sure most of them would spend alone, too. It was wonderful. We did a round-robin discussion of our emotional state and concerns. That party became the basis for a group that met monthly for more than a year. We called ourselves the FDWs (Fabulous Divorced Women)—and we were! As our needs dissipated and we strengthened, the group met less. Strong friendships and a lot of mutual support came out of the group. We still have an annual Father's Day get-together.

—Janie Jasin, Minnetonka, MN

SPECIAL OCCASIONS REQUIRING FAMILY TOGETHERNESS

There are many happy family occasions that should remain enjoyable. Sometimes events occur very soon after a family has separated and divorced, others occur sometime in the future. Now special considerations are required that never would have dawned on us B.D. (Before Divorce). Occasions such as graduations, confirmations, bar/bat mitzvahs, and weddings all benefit from cooperation on the part of both parents. These events were seldom easy to plan when you were all together. Now there are additional conflicts and considerations. Regardless, swords must be turned into plowshares for the occasion.

Financial cooperation varies greatly from family to family. "Fair" will be defined differently by each parent. Special occasions are an expense that falls outside of normal support payments. Even if one parent ends up paying for all or most of the event's festivities, keep in mind that a trade-off is that plans can be made to fit that parent's needs, tastes, and guest list. Regardless, the other parent should not be overlooked on such occasions, because your child will resent the other parent's absence. Ask your child for input when planning, and make your arrangements accordingly, even if it requires a lot of restraint on your part. Above all else, it is a day that should be one of good memories for your child.

If neither parent has remarried, you might talk about NOT inviting any significant (and especially, insignificant) others. Inevitably, one set of adults—if not both—will attend this occasion with a large knot in their respective stomachs. If one parent is now paired off and the other is not, there's all the more reason to avoid the uncomfortable feelings that are bound to surface. For the children to celebrate their occasion with only their original family is often nicest for them. And even if one parent has remarried, there is nothing wrong with that parent attending an occasion unpartnered, if it can reduce any tension levels for that special day. Obviously each family will deal with this in their own way but it is important to keep in mind that there are many ways . . . rather than just one way to celebrate such events. Family bonds do not go away simply because a divorce has taken place. It's not worth making them a test of any new marital connections.

Remember:

- Invitations can be worded as coming from the child to avoid the problem of which parent or parent's name to put on the invitation.
- You really don't have to do anything you don't want to do—despite traditions. You're never going to please everyone. When you plan the event, be sure that you are one of those to be pleased.

- If you can't stop being angry at your former or exiting spouse, fake it! Pretense is just fine. That doesn't mean that you must talk and socialize or even enjoy each others' company. Just be polite and civil.
- Discuss religious functions thoroughly with the participating clergy member. Some clergy may have their own desire for the *big happy family*. If you feel uncomfortable with their suggestions, you may need to talk with an "outsider" to keep your perspective.
- If you are planning to cooperate with another family, set time limits. ("If I don't hear from you by next Tuesday I will be ordering only XX invitations for the guests you wish to attend," is better than saying, "Please get back to me.")
- Keep it simple. The less you do, the fewer problems you'll have.

The other family brought their cameras into the sanctuary and took pictures. It drove me crazy but I had to let go of my feelings of anger. If they were inappropriate in their behavior, it did not reflect on me. I wasn't to blame and no one would consider me at fault—no matter how much it felt like that.
                    —Terri Newman, St. Louis Park, MN

Camp Visiting Days

Sleep-away camp for summer vacation is a choice of many single parents for their children. Be sure your camp director is sensitive to a child from a divorced family. Young children often have irrational concerns about their custodial parents disappearing. Extra contact is important. Write more, call regularly, and be there for visiting day.

Parents who may have cleared all the other hurdles

often find they have to communicate about sharing camp visiting days when they'd rather not. These are specific days and if you have to travel any distance, options to avoid each other are limited. But parents often forget that visiting days are hard on the kids— and maybe even harder than on the parents. Be sensitive to your children's reactions.

- Don't greet your child standing side-by-side with your ex. You don't want to put a child in the position of whom to hug first.
- Be sensitive to the other parent who may be taking video footage and probably doesn't want you on tape.

I knew he hated getting up early in the morning, so I'd arrive early and leave early. He'd arrive late and leave late.

—*Jill Saunders, Boca Raton, FL*

Boy-and-girl neighboring camps often allow divorced parents to visit each child alone, alternating Saturday and Sunday of that weekend. The parent of the same-gender child (i.e., mother/daughter and father/son) will have a seniority status at camp, because that parent can be in the bunk at any time, whereas the other parent can't. Most remote camps have only one nice hotel in the area. Only you can decide whether the comfort is worth the proximity to your ex-spouse. Similarly, when making a plane reservation, you can always check on the other's reservation by calling (and acting on your spouse's behalf) to confirm his or her reservation and then deciding which flight you'd like to take. Be creative. Your goal is to make your child feel loved without ruffling feathers unduly.

DATING, SEX, AND THE SINGLE PARENT

As most divorced adults eventually resume a social life, dating enters the picture. It is probably one of the more difficult things a child must become accustomed to. (It's not easy on you, either!) A child's usual reaction to Mom or Dad's first date is a negative one. Some divorced parents who've weathered the storms say, "Make sure the first date you bring home is a *throwaway* rather than a *significant* one. A child *never* likes the first one."

Rushing into dating threatens a child's world. Your children may view your dates as competition for your love and attention and as a rejection of their other, now-absent parent. Their fantasies of reconciliation will be damaged; and the loss of your attention can reawaken fears of abandonment. Beware of letting yourself think that finding a new spouse will make your family "whole" again. Remarriage based on that agenda often has more "holes" than "wholes." Be aware, too, that children are usually more accepting of Dad's dating than of Mom's dating. It's hard to say whether it's a sexist reaction or just that Mom, more often than not, is the caretaking parent and is expected to maintain the status quo.

Socializing with your kids along is one good way to approach the social scene. *Parents Without Partners* is a large, national organization that allows you this option. Or start your own family-to-family social group. It's really not hard. Invite all your single-with-children friends over for some shared event, such as a brunch. Socializing with your kids takes the pressure off of meeting "someone" because you can always enjoy being there with your child(ren). If you think you don't know enough folks in the category, simply let friends invite friends or acquaintances they may have heard about. Your network just needs a little nudge.

FINDING OTHER SINGLE PARENTS

There are friends, personal ads, dating services, singles groups, and clubs, to name just a few ways to meet other singles. Being single is a wonderful opportunity to meet people you don't have to marry. You've already been married and have had kids. You did what society expected of you. Now you can meet new people—and pair off or not as is appropriate—without a mating agenda. There are wonderful single women and men who would love to know you. Enjoy the opportunity. And if it's love you're looking for, remember you have to kiss a lot of toads before you find your prince or princess. It's mainly a percentage game!

PARENTS WITHOUT PARTNERS. Perhaps the best-known of the organized singles groups, with 1200 local chapters in the United States and Canada offers discussion groups, workshops, children's programs, and social events. They publish a bimonthly magazine. For information write to: 8807 Colesville Rd., Silver Spring, MD, or call 1-301-588-9354.

For most, dating and sex the second time around is scary and stressful. Just because you've been married doesn't mean you're confident or are even experienced in this area. Becoming socially active again is important because it helps free a parent from becoming obsessive about his or her parenting role. Letting your adult life revolve around your child's is actually very hard on your child. To help out, here are some dating do's and don'ts:

- Meet your dates away from home in the beginning of a new relationship.

- Introduce dates as friends if your child resents your dating, explaining that parents need adult friends, too. Add a tag such as "so-and-so is my tennis partner," or "a co-worker from the office."
- Try not to have a slew of different dates running through your home and your child's life. This lifestyle might be fun for you, but it's confusing for and hard on children.
- Enjoy the benefits of shared physical custody, if you have it. You can perhaps confine your dating to the times the children are not with you. If you only have access to your children on weekends, there will come a point when they have to share in your dating life. Just remember that the longer this takes, the easier it will be for your children.
- Begin locking a bedroom door for privacy before you have someone spending the night so that option is available to you.
- Choose with care those *significant others* whom you let get close to your family. Children get attached to people you date over a long period of time, and these breakups are often harder on them than on the adults involved.
- Letting your ex know your whereabouts when going out of town is a responsible act, but is not always done. If your ex will not give you a phone number, suggest that he or she let you know who does know how to reach him should an emergency arise. (This is not the same as keeping tabs on your former spouse's social life—consciously or unconsciously.)

You are not the first divorced person to feel or experience anything that is surprising you. One of the best "we've-been-there-too" books is *Living and Loving After Divorce*, by C. Napolitane (NAL), founder of Nexus, a support network devoted to helping divorced women start their new lives (*see page 243*).

Be prepared when your children attempt to sabotage your dates through a variety of rude comments, obnoxious behavior, and "forgetting" to pass on phone messages. You can let a child know that you understand what he or she is feeling, but make it clear that this type of behavior is unacceptable. As for your sex life, do recognize that despite their knowledge and savvy, children are usually uncomfortable with their parents' sexuality. It's not necessary to reveal the sexual component of any relationship, at least until some commitment seems to be in the offing. You can avoid forcing your child to deal with this by taking an overnight trip, going to a hotel, or waiting until you have some privacy in your own home.

If spending the night with a date, I'd always tell the kids I would not be home, though not necessarily where I was. It was important to me to let the kids never think I might be deserting them.
                                                    —Unsigned

---

Time is your best ally. Don't be in a hurry to have your children participate in your relationships. If you find yourself feeling uneasy about having your "friend" stay overnight while your kids are around, don't issue the invitation. Many parents go to elaborate lengths to keep their love life private, even when their children are in the house with them. There are as many solutions to finding private times as there are single parents. Be prepared, also, for surprising questions about your marital and premarital love life. Your kids may want to know whether you and Mom (Dad) slept together before you were married, whether you were monogamous in marriage, or how many partners you may have had. Be as honest as you feel is appropriate.

Teens, especially, may be looking for reasons to say no to peer pressure, so make your answers constructive for them.

The first male I had over for dinner had to deal with my six-year-old daughter asking, "Are you going to marry my mommy?" "No," he replied, "I'm going to wait and marry you!"

—Susan Beatty, New Canaan, CT

If your love life isn't so hot, it can be agonizing to see your ex dating or in love. One underlying reason for your pain, as we all feel when uncoupled, is fear that WE'LL never be loved again. It's not true. Love comes when you least expect it. It arrives on its own timetable, not yours. It often comes after your heart has healed or when finding a partner is no longer a consuming objective.

But You're in Love

The first time you do expose your kids to your love life there will probably be some uneasy feelings no matter how well everyone is prepared. Some parents discuss this possibility with their kids beforehand to help form their decision and/or timing; afterward is still time enough to ask your kids how they felt about your having an overnight guest. It's a difficult situation because we want our children to see an honest, loving relationship that they can use for a model, but may be ambivalent or downright worried about their "getting the wrong ideas"—or even carrying your "news" to an ex-spouse. Then too, even seeing adults holding hands and kissing affectionately may add to kids' embarrassment and confusion, rather than clarifying it. A love-struck adult who behaves like an adolescent blurs the necessary differences between the adult-child relationship. Share your giggles, passionate excitement, or pining with friends—out of earshot of your children.

One study reports that divorced mothers living with men complicated their children's adjustment. The kids don't fare as well because they believe the new relationship to be tenuous and they're unsure of the other man's role. Kids are often embarrassed when their mothers have live-in lovers. And if they do become fond of the new man in Mom's life, they are often torn by a sense of disloyalty to their absent father. And children resent—and understandably so—being told what to do by someone who is not their parent. This is true whether you are dating or are remarried.

Remember that whatever standard you expect of your children, you will have to live up to yourself. Teens are not going to be content to "do as I say, not as I do." Dating does give you the opportunity to help shape your children's dating standards. If they see you having dates or friendships that don't necessarily involve sex, hear how you talk about your dates and what you like and don't like about them, learn how you treat a date by where you go/how you are treated, you can help them form appropriate dating values and behavior.

Beware of the pitfall of abandoning your children emotionally when a significant other comes into the picture. Nurturing children often falls to the wayside in the flush of a romance. If you have developed a close relationship with your child or children when you were alone, your new couple relationship will threaten your parent-child relationship. Children will find ways to cope with a loss of attention. It might be negative behavior, withdrawing from the family, or even making an ally of this new person.

Time alone with your children becomes even more

important when a couple relationship takes shape. Children usually resent lack of one-on-one time when visiting a parent who has a date. Finding a balance is difficult; no adult wants to spend all weekend, every weekend in the company of a 5- or 7-year-old. But the other extreme, that of having the children share all of a parent's time with another adult, competing for attention, is very hard on the children.

Since my mom has married again, she's so much in love that I'm just in the way.

—*16-year-old daughter*

So Your Ex Is in Love

So you don't like his or her new date. There is nothing you can do about having your child(ren) visit when your ex has a friend sleep over. It may be hard emotionally but you have to live with it. There is nothing that you should *say* about this, either. Feelings of being replaced by another woman or man are normal, albeit irrational. Children's sexual mores and values are not corrupted by such situations, if that is your concern.

When your ex's date becomes the mate, you may be surprised at how painful the prospect is—even when you have no wish to reconcile. The best explanation is that it seems to be yet another and even more final reminder that your marriage has ended.

Remarriage

A second marriage brings about a whole new set of considerations, as does step-parenting, if that's part of the new marriage. Fifty percent of those divorced with children will remarry. Obviously, you shouldn't contemplate remarriage just so your kids can have a full-time, live-in mother or father; second marriages fail at a higher rate than first marriages. More people are currently single or remarried than are part of an intact family. Thirty-five percent of American children now live in a step relationship, and it is predicted that 75 percent of all step relations will break up. These are sobering statistics. Seek family counseling *before* you remarry or merge families so you know what you will be facing and can develop some tools to use before problems arise. Discussion of topics such as discipline, money, inheritance, adoption of children, and custody concerns if divorce occurs again are just some that need to be covered. Think of pre-second-marriage counseling as taking out an insurance policy.

Remember, single parenting has many untouted advantages. Go slow. Marriage, as you may recall, seldom solves more problems than it creates. Children are generally better off, studies are showing, in one-parent families than in new "blended" families. Kids have fewer behavior problems when their divorced parents stayed single than when they reconcile or when the custodial parent remarried.

Remarriage and step-parenting are topics that require whole books to themselves, and many have been written. If you are taking the plunge, use the books and resources available. Don't think that love conquers all—you should know better from your first divorce.

Beware of the Family Ties that Blind

When remarriage occurs, adults often bring to that relationship the desire for it to contain all the rights, responsibilities, and respect that is granted first time around for themselves and their new partner. A new

---

SECOND TIME AROUND

THE STEPFAMILY ASSOCIATION OF AMERICA
602 E. Joppa Rd.
Baltimore, MD 21204
(301)823-7570
They have a book catalog, a quarterly newsletter, and
sponsor chapters across the country.

THE STEPFAMILY FOUNDATION
333 West End Ave.
New York, NY 10023
(212)877-3244
They offer counseling seminars, an information clearinghouse, and a quarterly newsletter.

---

wife, for instance, is expected to attend a family occasion despite the discomfort it may cause her and everyone else. If one spouse says, "Accept me, accept
my new partner," it may prove to be a painful point of
honor. Keep in mind that there can be a place for old
family ties and a place for new family ties that can (if
you can accept this type of thinking) make it easier for
all concerned. Every event doesn't *have* to be a paired
affair. Be flexible. Keep in mind everyone's comfort
level on special occasions, especially the thoughts and
needs of the child who will either miss your presence
or face any added anxiety.

RELIGIOUS CLOSURE

Marriage is a legal and, for many couples, a religious
contract. The legal aspect of divorce deals only with
practical details of custody and property. Many who
divorce feel the need for a religious "closure" cere-

mony as well. It helps them to counter the emotional pain suffered by both the adults and children involved.

For Jews

The Jewish religion has as part of its tradition a divorce ceremony called the "get," which is also the name of the divorce document. The traditional ceremony is somewhat sexist in nature, because only the husband can divorce the wife, not vice versa. Other branches of Judaism have modified this ceremony to make it more meaningful for women who wish to include it in their divorce. The Reform branch has the "Ritual of Release," which can be performed with a couple or just one spouse, if the other is uncooperative.

For Catholics

For the Catholic, the official process for religious closure is that of annulment. Catholics can take advantage of this process by contacting the parish priest or local Tribunal office. The process of annulment, which can only occur after a civil divorce, allows Catholics to reconsider the religious, sacramental nature of their marriage. The process takes six months to a year, and requires a person to work with their parish priest or a lay field advocate before a local Tribunal will support any conclusive judgment on the sacramental nature of that marriage. A church decision never denies the fact that there was a civil marriage. For that reason, a degree of nullity never makes children born to that marriage illegitimate. Instead, the decision focuses on the emotional and ethical considerations of marriage and divorce.

For an informative discussion on annulment, send for a copy of the Catholic Update brochure: "Why the

Church Is Granting More Annulments" (#CU-1080) by sending 50 cents to St. Anthony Messenger Press, 1615 Republic St., Cincinnati, OH 45210.

For Non-Catholic Christians

The United Church of Christ in 1987 became the first U.S. Christian body to authorize a ritual recognition for divorce. The UCC's *Book of Worship* now includes a five-page "Order of Recognition of the End of a Marriage" to be conducted after a civil divorce. This includes the couple's participation in a rite in which they recite words of regret and respect.

Whether children will participate in these ceremonies is a personal decision for both adults and children. Religious closure helps deal with the spiritual and psychological aspect of divorce. It's about the only public acknowledgment of a divorce our society offers. But it's important to remember that closure, even with a religious component, is never quite final when there are children.

It was something I wanted to do but really couldn't at first. We were both finally ready about four years after our divorce. Despite my Reform Jewish affiliation, a Reform "get" isn't recognized by the Conservative or Orthodox branches and I wanted it to be done in everyone's eyes—regardless—so we had the Orthodox ceremony. I didn't have the children present as this was my thing, not theirs. During the procedure, I had a powerful flashback to our ring ceremony that had now come full circle. I was hit by the loss of that earlier dream. Later I sobbed and sobbed. It was a significant act of closure for me.
—Tamara Kaiser, Chevy Chase, MD

Afterword

If you have made it to the end of this book, I'm impressed. Reading and concentration are no easy task when you're in the process of a divorce.

What seems like the end now for you is really only the beginning. Trust me, it's true. Your emotional roller-coaster ride will end and your new insights will buoy you. There is a light at the end of this dark tunnel. It's the glow from inside of you that will light up your life anew.

WHAT LIES BEHIND US AND
WHAT LIES BEFORE US ARE
TINY MATTERS COMPARED TO
WHAT LIES WITHIN US.

Sources

REFERENCES FOR PREFACE, CHAPTER 1

"Children Who Cope in Spite of Divorce," by Judith Wallerstein, *Family Advocate Journal*, Summer 1978.

"Divorce: Do It for the Kids?" by Jeff Meer, *Psychology Today*, July 1987, p. 22.

"Containing the Pain," *Working Mother*, July 1987, p. 18.

"Research Reveals Many Former Relationships Positive," *Marriage & Divorce Today* Newsletter, November 4, 1985.

Surviving the Breakup: How Children Cope with Divorce, by Judith Wallerstein and Joan Kelly, Basic Books, 1980.

REFERENCES FOR CHAPTER 2

Anna Weintraub, from *Working Mother*, October 1983, "When Kids Have Grown-up Worries."

"Stressful Family Syndrome" from *The New York Times*, February, 1986.

"Post-divorce: Phasing In," by Neala Schwartzberg, Ph.D., *Working Parents*, Oct./Nov. 1985.

Linda Franke, *San Francisco Chronicle*, July 1983.

Growing up Divorced: Help Your Child Through the Stages, by Linda Franke, Simon & Schuster, 1983.

"Joint and Maternal Custody, the Outcome for Boys Aged 6–11 and Their Parents," by Virginia Shiller. Paper presented at the 62d Annual Meeting of the American Orthopsychiatric Association, New York, April 24, 1985.

"Emotional Adjustment of Boys in Sole Custody and Joint Custody Compared with Adjustment of Boys in Happy and Unhappy Marriages," by Everett G. Pojman. Doctoral dissertation, California Graduate Institute.

How to Survive Your Kids, by Joseph Novello, M.D., McGraw-Hill, 1988.

"Father Custody and Social Development in Boys and Girls," by John W. Santrock and Richard A. Warshak, *Journal of Social Issues,* vol. 35, no. 4, 1979.

Bob Brancle, October 1985 issue of *Family Relations.*

"Understanding Key to Helping Teenagers Cope With Parents' Divorce," AAP's *Young Health,* Summer 1986.

"Helping Teens Cope With Parental Divorce," *Pediatric News,* August 1984.

Parent Education and Intervention Handbook, Richard A. Abiden (ed.), Charles C. Thomas, 1980.

REFERENCES FOR CHAPTER 4

Barbara Mindel, "Divorce and the Teen," the July 1986 issue of *Welcome Home* with permission of the author.

Divorce Happens to the Nicest Kids, by Michael Prokop, Alegra House, Warren, OH, 1986.

REFERENCES FOR CHAPTER 5

"Taxes in Splitsville," *Consumer Reports*, March 1988.

Minneapolis Star Tribune, April 28, 1988.

"Average Child Support Payment Drops by 12.4%," *The New York Times* (AP), August 23, 1987, p. 15.

"Crisis in Family Law: Children as Victims of Divorce," National Council for Children's Rights, 1986.

"Child Custody, Child Support Arrangements and Child Support Payment Patterns," by Jessica Pearson and Nancy Thoennes, Association of Family and Conciliation Courts, Denver, CO, 1985.

Abduction (.7) *Growing Child Research Review*, September 1986, Dunn & Hargitt, Lafayette, IN.

Marianne Takas, *Child Custody*, Harper & Row Publishers, Inc., 1987.

The Disposable Parent, by Mel Roman et al., 1978, Holt Rinehart & Winston.

Stepfamilies and Beyond Newsletter, 1988, Gary, IN.

When All Else Fails, by Ronald Supancic with D. L. Baker, Fleming Revell, 1986.

"Parental Kidnapping, Parents Guide to Prevention and Recovery," Hutt Communications, Box 70366, Fort Lauderdale, FL 33307.

Parent Education and Intervention Handbook, Richard R. Abiden (ed.), Charles C. Thomas, 1980.

"Lines on World Map Bar Mother from Children," by Tamar Lewin, *The New York Times*, July 31, 1988.

REFERENCES FOR CHAPTER 6

"Learning From Single Dads," by Dennis Meredith, *Twins Magazine*, March/April 1986.

"Father Custody and Social Development in Boys and Girls," by John W. Santrock and Richard A. Warsak, *Journal of Social Issues*, vol. 35, no. 4, 1979.

"Noncustodial Mothers Who Do Not Feel Guilty," *Behavior Today*, December 7, 1987.

How to Survive Your Kids, by Joseph Novello, M.D., McGraw-Hill, 1988.

Ellen Goodman, © 1977, The Boston Globe Newspaper Company/Washington Post Writers Group. Reprinted with permission.

"Synopsis of Sole and Joint Custody Studies," National Council for Children's Rights, 1987.

Child Support, Kahn, Alfred J., and Sheila B. Kamerman, eds., Sage Publications, 1988, p. 318.

"Crisis in Family Law: Children as Victims of Divorce," National Council for Children's Rights, 1986, p. 12.

"Sixty Rapid-Fire Points in Favor of Joint Custody," National Council for Children's Rights, 1986.

Marriage and Divorce Today Newsletter, May 1985.

"The Debate Over Joint Custody," by Marilyn Webb, *Working Women*, May 1986, p. 162.

"Can It Work When Parents Don't Get Along?" MDT Newsletter, March 16, 1987.

"Learning From Single Dads," by Dennis Meredith, *Twins Magazine*, March/April 1986.

Sandra Pope's "Learning to Live with Co-Parenting" (July/Aug 1987),© TWINS Magazine, Inc. Reprinted with permission of *Twins Magazine*, P.O. Box 12045, Overland Park, KS 66212.

REFERENCES FOR CHAPTER 7

The Mothers' Book: Shared Experiences, by Richard Friedland and Carol Kort, Houghton Mifflin, 1981.

"The Relationship of School Achievement and Disciplinary Problems to Single Parent Families Among Selected Tenth and Twelfth Grade Students," by Robert Mengerink, University of Akron, 1987.

Ellen Goodman, *The Boston Globe*, January 26, 1988.

Living Alone and Liking It, by Lynn Shahan, Warner Books, 1981.

"Kids Troubled by Mom's Live-In Lover" (Maria Isaacs of Families of Divorce Project), reported by Karen Peterson, *USA Today*, October 24, 1986.

"Guidelines for Nurturing Children After Divorce," by John and Emily Visher, *Nurturing Today*, Winter 1987/88, San Francisco, CA.

"Most Find Christmas Alone to Be the Hardest," by Vicki Lansky, *Minneapolis Star Tribune*, December 23, 1984.

"Single Parents and Dating," by Andree Brooks, *The New York Times*, September 16, 1985.

"Teens, Divorce and the Holidays," by Claire Costello, *Parents Press*, Oakland, CA, 1985.

"Life After Divorce Filled with Problems for Kids," by Connie Denham, *Stepfamily Bulletin*, Summer 1985.

Sally Brush, Aring Institute, Cincinnati, OH, 1988.

"Why Children of Divorce Fare Poorly in School," *Marriage & Divorce Today* Newsletter, October 13, 1986.

"The Second Time Around," *Working Mother*, July 1988.

Additional Reading

BOOKSHELF ON DIVORCE

A Selection of Bestselling Books to Help You Through the Transition of Your Divorce

For you:

CREATIVE DIVORCE, by M. Krantzler (Signet). A classic primer by a therapist that can help anyone begin to deal with the crisis of their divorce. A positive program of action! $4.95

CRAZY TIME: SURVIVING DIVORCE, by A. Trafford (Bantam). The author takes you through the stages of crisis, craziness AND finally recovery that will help you understand your OWN behavior. $4.50

THE DIVORCE HANDBOOK: YOUR BASIC GUIDE, by J. Friedman (Random House). A specialist in family law covers the legal aspects of a divorce so you can understand your rights and your responsibilities. $7.95

THE DOLLARS & SENSE OF DIVORCE, by J. Briles (Master Media). Take control of your financial life from negotiating child/spousal support, locating and defining assets and understanding the money game. $10.95

LIVING AND LOVING AFTER DIVORCE, by C. Napolitane (Signet). A warm, supportive women's guide to men, dating, personal growth and more. $4.95

For your emotional health:

HOW TO SURVIVE THE LOSS OF A LOVE, by Colgrove, et al. (Bantam). A wonderful collection of readings for overcoming hurt and loss felt during divorce. $3.95

DIVORCE: THE PAIN AND THE HEALING, by J. Mattis. A collection of meditations on the end of a marriage to aid the healing process during crisis, separation and readjustment. $6.50

NO HIDDEN MEANINGS, by S. Kopp (Science & Behavior). Inspirational photo essay of "truths" about the human condition to keep the pain in perspective. $8.95

BREAKING UP: FROM HEARTACHE TO HAPPINESS IN 48 PAGES, by Y. Nave (Workman). If laughter is the best medicine, this illustrated book is just the remedy you need. $3.50

For parenting during divorce:

MOM'S HOUSE, DAD'S HOUSE: MAKING SHARED CUSTODY WORK, by I. Ricci (Collier). A book that will help with the everyday considerations that can make joint custody a successful option. $7.95

HELPING CHILDREN COPE WITH SEPARATION AND LOSS, by C. Jewett (Harvard Common). Children grieve too. Learn about the expected behavior of the mourning process and learn techniques that help children process their losses. $8.95

For your children to read:

WHERE IS DADDY? THE STORY OF A DIVORCE, by B. Goff (Beacon Press). This is the story of Janeydear whose parents divorce and how she begins to understand her feelings of confusion and fear and how she resolves them. (For ages 3–6) $4.95

THE DINOSAURS DIVORCE, by L. & M. Brown (Little, Brown). Dinosaurs who marry must also deal with divorce. Playful, colored illustrations deal with the various aspects of divorce from visitation to telling friends. The book suggests positive ways to handle new situations and difficulties that divorce brings. (For ages 4–8) $4.95

WHY ARE WE GETTING A DIVORCE? by P. Mayle (Crown). With a blend of humor, sensitivity and full color illustrations, this book covers many topics with sympathy and reassurance; from adjusting to living with one parent to dealing with feelings of hurt and loss. (For ages 6–12) $11.95

HOW IT FEELS WHEN PARENTS DIVORCE, by J. Krementz (Knopf). The author/photographer interviews boys and girls from seven to sixteen about the feelings experienced when their parents separated and divorced. (For children ages 8–14) $8.95

IT'S NOT THE END OF THE WORLD, by J. Blume (Dell). An easy-to-read novel about a 12-year-old, middle child of three, who takes on the impossible task of getting her separated parents back together again. Her brother runs away and her sister becomes withdrawn. Once the divorce and the fighting ends, the children settle in. They realize that life's not all that bad after all. (For ages 9–12) $2.95

Call or write to:
The Book Peddlers, Dept D-NAL,
Deephaven, MN 55391
1-800-255-3379
Ask for free catalogue of other books by VICKI LANSKY

Index